LATE HAN CHINESE

This book continues and carries a stage further Professor Dobson's pioneering researches into the nature and development of Classical Chinese. He has here compared a Late Archaic text with a paraphrase of that text written in Late Han Chinese. From that comparison he describes in systematic detail the changes that occur in Classical Chinese in the intervening five hundred years. These changes, unlike the changes that take place between Early and Middle and Middle and Late Archaic Chinese, which are formal only, show a fundamental shift. The "empty words" of Classical Chinese which, in Archaic Chinese, are crucial as grammatical indicators, in Late Han become, as later philologists have traditionally described them, "full words." Many Archaic particles become obsolete in Late Han. The "full words" in Late Han, by contrast, perform a more predictable grammatical function. Periphrastic forms replace "participles" for negation, mood, voice, and the like. "Full words" tend towards compounding and to greater restriction in syntactical deployment. This change Professor Dobson characterizes as "the Archaic-Han Shift." The Archaic-Han Shift anticipates features of the Chinese language which are familiar in Modern Standard Chinese.

This book contains, in addition, appendices describing the notions of Late Han scholars about language, the differences between "classical" and "literary" Chinese in the Late Han period, and features of Late Han which anticipate grammatical features of Modern Standard Chinese.

Late Han Chinese, together with the author's earlier works, *Late Archaic Chinese* and *Early Archaic Chinese*, constitutes a significant chapter of research in the history and development of the Chinese language. Each contains a lexicon of grammatical particles for its respective period. *Late Han Chinese* will take its place, together with its predecessors, as a standard reference work for all future students of the Chinese language.

W.A.C.H. DOBSON is Professor of Chinese in the Department of East Asian Studies, University of Toronto. He is a graduate in Oriental Studies of Oxford, and the degree of Doctor of Letters was conferred on him recently by that University.

LATE

HAN CHINESE

—

A Study of the Archaic-Han Shift

W. A. C. H. DOBSON

Professor of Chinese and Head of the Department
of East Asian Studies, University of Toronto

—

UNIVERSITY OF TORONTO PRESS

© University of Toronto Press 1964

Reprinted in paperback 2015

ISBN 978-0-8020-1308-8 (cloth)

ISBN 978-1-4426-3117-5 (paper)

à

PAUL DEMIÉVILLE

Doyen des Sinologues

PREFACE

In writing this book, as with <u>Late Archaic Chinese</u>
and <u>Early Archaic Chinese</u>, to which it is complementary,
I have enjoyed the benefit of the advice of a number of
scholars, too many to acknowledge in person. I gratefully record my thanks to them. I must, however,
particularly thank Mr. A.H.C. Ward for valuable observations drawn from his own researches on the <u>Leu-shyh
Chuen-chiou</u>, which he has allowed me to include. I am
also indebted to Mrs. Betty Easterbrook who typed the
manuscript and to Raymond Chu who wrote the Chinese
characters.

This volume is a companion to <u>Late Archaic Chinese</u>
and to <u>Early Archaic Chinese</u>. It has, however, been
reproduced from typewritten manuscript by the photo-
offset process, because of the peculiar difficulty of
procuring the Chinese type necessary, and the consequent
delay involved in using Chinese type.

I gratefully acknowledge the financial assistance
provided by the Humanities Research Fund of the University of Toronto.

Finally in homage to Professor Paul Demiéville of
the Collège de France, on his completing fifty years in
the service of Sinology, this book is, with permission,
respectfully dedicated to him.

W.A.C.H. Dobson

Massey College,
University of Toronto.
1964

CONTENTS

PREFACE   vii

INTRODUCTION   xiii

  (i) Aims and Objects   xiii
 (ii) History of the Study   xiii
(iii) Late Han Literary Chinese   xvii
 (iv) Method and Statement   xx
  (v) Method and Procedure   xxi
 (vi) The Archaic Han Shift   xxiii

1.   THE ARCHAIC-HAN SHIFT   3

2.   SYNTAGMA   4

  2.1. The Personal Pronouns   4
     i. Obsolescence of Determinative Forms   4
  2.2. The Anaphoric Pronouns   5
     i. The Blunting of Distinctions   5
  2.3. The Demonstratives   6
     i. Obsolescence of Determinative Forms   6
     ii. Chyi as a Demonstrative   7
     iii. Chyi in Chyi-shyr etc.   8
     iv. Chyi before Ren   8
  2.4. Collectives and Restrictives   9
     i. Shift in meaning of Farn   9
     ii. Dann before Nouns   10
  2.5. The Particle of Syntagma   11
     i. Jee as a marker of Cause   11
  2.6. The Particle of Determination   11
     i. Blunting of usage   11
  2.7. Syntagma in Summary   12

3.   THE VERB   14

  3.1. Mood   14
     i. The reduction of the role of the
       Modal Negatives to negation   14
     ii. The blunting of the Modal Negatives   16
     iii. Stressed or Intensive Negatives are
       replaced by periphrastic forms   16
     iv. Modification in meaning of Wey   17
     v. The blunting of the Modal role of
       Guoo and Guh   18
     vi. The replacement of Yeou and Wei in
       the Subjunctive   19

      vii. The marking of the Injunctive   20
      viii. The use of Shiu and Ing   21
      ix. The modal functions of Kee and Neng   23
   3.2. Aspect   23
      i. Shifts in Potential and Momentary Aspect   23
      ii. Perfective Aspect   24
      iii. The use of Fuh for Durative and
           Iterative Aspect   25
      iv. Dann and Aspect   26
      v. Dann and Polarity   27
      vi. The use of Jyi and Biann   29
      vii. The use of Meei and Jer   30
   3.3. Manner   31
      i. The misinterpretation of Yan   31
      ii. The interpretation of 'yeou-attribute'
          and 'attribute/sy'   32
   3.4. Voice   32
      i. The Jiann Passive   33
      ii. The Bey Passive   34
      iii. The Periphrastic Passive in Wei   35
      iv. Causative and permissive   36
      v. Tzay as a post-verbal particle   37
   3.5. Direction   38
      i. Tzyh is replaced by Tsorng   38
      ii. You is replaced by Tsorng   39
   3.6. Polarity   39
      i. The obsolescence of the polar form
         'negative/substitute/verb'   39
      ii. Dann and Polarity   40
   3.7. The Verb in Summary   41

4. AGENCY   44

   4.1. The Pronouns   44
      i. Obsolescence of the agentive forms
         of the Pronouns   44
   4.2. The Distributives   45
      i. The obsolescence of Huoh and Moh   45
      ii. The encroachment of Jiu upon Jie
          and Jie   47
      iii. Jiu as a Collective   48
      iv. Shwu is assimilated into Shwei   48
      v. The use of Shyan   48
   4.3. Reciprocity   49
      i. The obsolescence of Jiau and the
         parasitic use of Shiang   49
   4.4. Delegated Agency   50
      i. Wey encroaches upon Wey   50
   4.5. The Reflexive   51
      i. The use of Tzyh in compounds   51

        ii. The use of the Emphatic and Reflexive
            Pronoun Jii   52
    4.6. Agency in Summary   54

5. CLAUSES, PHRASES AND ENDINGS IN THE
    VERBAL SENTENCE   56

    5.1. The Erl Clause   56
        i. Diminution in the role of Erl   56
        ii. The use of the Jih Clause   58
    5.2. The Instrumental   58
        i. Erl terminating the Instrumental Clause   58
    5.3. Anaphora   59
        i. The use of Anaphora   59
        ii. The eroding of the Anaphoric Pronouns
            in allegro forms   61
    5.4. The Final Particles   64
        i. The loss of precision   64
        ii. The use of Foou and Ran   65
        iii. Foou and Bu as final interrogatives   66
    5.5. Time and Place   67
        i. Shyi becomes obsolescent   67
        ii. Miscellaneous   67
    5.6. The Verbal Sentence in Summary   69

6. THE DETERMINATIVE SENTENCE   71

    6.1. The Copulae   71
        i. Shyh as a Copula   71
        ii. Dann as a Copula   72
        iii. Jyi as a Copula   72
        iv. The Compounding of the Copulae of
            Common Inclusion   73
    6.2. Cause and Consequence   73
        i. The use of Yuan   73
    6.3. The Determinative Sentence in Summary   74

7. CONJUNCTIONS   75

    7.1. Co-ordinate sequence   75
        i. Fuh as a Co-ordinate Conjunction   75
        ii. The Adversative   76
        iii. The use of Faan "on the contrary"   77
    7.2. Conditioned Sequence   79
        (a) Marking the protasis   79
        i. Ru-shyy, ru, jea-shyy, and shyy   79
        ii. Cherng replaces Goou   80
        (b) Marking the apodosis   81
        iii. Tzer replaces Sy   81
        iv. Tzer replaced by Tsyy or Dang   81
        v. Jiow in Conditioned Sequences   81

7.3. Concession   82
    i. The use of Tzyh   82
    ii. Taang as a concessive conjunction   83
    iii. The use of Shanq in Concession   83
7.4. Conjunctions in Summary   85

8. SUBSTITUTION   87

8.1. The Pronouns   87
    i. The Personal Pronouns   87
    ii. The Anaphoric Pronouns   88
8.2. The Demonstratives   89
8.3. The Interrogative Substitutes   89
    i. The assimilation by An of Yan and
       U and U-hu   90
    ii. The use of Ninq   91
    iii. The assimilation of Shwu by Shwei   92
    iv. The obsolescence of Shi   92
    v. Expansions of LAC Her   92
    vi. Changes in the syntactical deployment
        of the Interrogative Substitutes   94
    vii. The use of Chii   94
    viii. The use of Tserng   95
8.4. Substitution in Summary   95

9. MISCELLANEOUS   97

1. The Degrees of Comparison   97
2. The Allegro Forms   99
3. Enumeration   99
4. Miscellaneous in Summary   100

10. CONCLUSION   101

POSTSCRIPT   103

APPENDIXES

    I. Late Han and Early Archaic Chinese   105
    II. The Nature of Late Han Classical Chinese   109
    III. Late Han and Modern Standard Chinese   112
    IV. Jaw Chyi's notions about Language   115

LIST OF WORKS MENTIONED   119

INDEX OF WORDS TREATED AT SOME LENGTH   121

INTRODUCTION

(i) Aims and Objects

The present work is a comparative study of the grammar of two stages in the evolution of "Classical Chinese." More particularly, it is a detailed study of a 3rd Century B.C. text (Late Archaic Chinese) and of a paraphrase of that text in the language of the 2nd Century A.D. (Late Han Literary Chinese). The comparison is made in an attempt to explore the nature of evolutionary change in the language, by comparing samples of two periods which have a common subject-matter. If these two samples prove to be typical, and there is good reason to think that they are,[1] then a fundamental shift occurs in the language between Late Archaic and Late Han. It is the purpose of the present work to describe that shift - - the Archaic-Han-Shift - - as a contribution towards an historical treatment of the grammar of Archaic and Classical Chinese.

(ii) History of the Study

The present study is a continuation of, and a further stage in, a long-term programme of research. This programme began with an attempt to devise a purely formal system for describing the grammar of Archaic Chinese. The system was then applied, period by period, in a series of diachronic descriptive grammars of Archaic Chinese. Three periods were set up: Early, Middle and Late Archaic Chinese. By comparing the variables period by period, the rough shape of evolutionary change within Archaic Chinese was then sketched. The present study

---

[1] See paragraph iii below.

adds a further period - - Late Han, and a further set
of variables - - the differences observable by these
methods between Late Archaic and Late Han Literary
Chinese. At a further stage, it is proposed to add
more periods and to make further comparisons. At an
ultimate stage, the periodization can be refined, the
changes more closely observed,[2] even accurately dated,
and the study will then culminate in a synchronic
Grammar of Classical Chinese - - from its "classical"
beginnings to the wide variety of forms which, though
patterned on classical models, in fact emerged, and
comprise what is generically called "Classical Chinese."

    The present study is thus only meaningful when
taken with its predecessors. In Late Archaic Chinese[3]
the possibility of describing the grammar of Archaic
Chinese by strictly formal and observable criteria was
explored. Analytical procedure was based on the ob-
servation that the Archaic Chinese "word" (which is in-
capable of inflexion or of change of "phonological
shape"),[4] varies in its reference and function as it
assumes various relationships with other "words."
Classes were set up in terms of sets of relationships - -

----

    [2] See postscript.

----

    [3] W.A.C.H. Dobson, Late Archaic Chinese (Toronto
1959), abbreviated hereafter as LAC.

----

    [4] With the exception of phonological change at the
lexical level as a process of word derivation, see LAC
Appendix 1.

"frames" or "matrices" - - in which the otherwise un-
changing word can be observed to occur.[5]

In LAC this system was applied in presenting a diachronic description of the grammar of a sampling of
Archaic Chinese authors of the 4th and 3rd Centuries
B.C. This language was characterized as Late Archaic
Chinese (= LAC). In Early Archaic Chinese[6] the degree
of predictability of the system was tested by applying
it to a corpus of bronze inscriptions of the 11th and
10th Centuries B.C. The language of these inscriptions
has hitherto been little understood. This language,
characterized as Early Archaic Chinese (= EAC), is also
the language of the Wuu Gaw (五誥), traditionally
thought to be the "most genuine" of the books of the
Shu Jing.

In an Appendix to EAC[7] features of EAC and LAC were
placed side by side in order to explore the nature of
evolutionary change in the language from the 11th-10th
Centuries to the 4th-3rd Centuries B.C. Further, by

_____

[5] See "Word Classes or Distributional Classes in
Archaic Chinese"; in "L'Hommage à Monsieur Demiéville"
(in press).

_____

[6] W.A.C.H. Dobson, Early Archaic Chinese (Toronto
1962), abbreviated hereafter as EAC.

_____

[7] EAC Appendix 1, "Towards a Historical Treatment
of the Grammar of Archaic Chinese."

making a diachronic descriptive study of the <u>Spring and Autumn Annals</u>[8] - - a text poised in time somewhere between EAC and LAC and set up provisionally as Middle Archaic Chinese (=MAC) - - it was possible to explore the nature of evolutionary change further. With the features of three samplings of three periods within Archaic Chinese compared, discernible shifts and changes were apparent as the language progresses from Early to Middle and from Middle to Late Archaic Chinese. These shifts and changes were examined in depth and detail in a study of one grammatical feature in an article "Early Archaic <u>yüeh</u> > Late Archaic <u>chi</u>."[9] In the present study the process of taking samples of periodical "cuts" in the language and submitting them to analysis and comparison has been continued.

The present study therefore assumes the postulates of previous studies.[10] The system of analysis, its terminology, the "sampling method," the organization of the

---

[8] W.A.C.H. Dobson, "Studies in Middle Archaic Chinese - - The Spring and Autumn Annals," <u>T'oung Pao</u> (1963) L. 1-3, pp. 221-238.

---

[9] W.A.C.H. Dobson "Towards a Historical Treatment of the Grammar of Archaic Chinese - - Early Archaic Yüeh > Late Archaic <u>Chi</u>," <u>HJAS</u> 23 (1961) pp. 5-18.

---

[10] To the above-mentioned studies should be added: W.A.C.H. Dobson, "Studies in the Grammar of Early Archaic Chinese, I, The Particle <u>Wei</u>," <u>T'oung Pao</u> XLVI (1958) pp. 339-368; and "Studies in the Grammar of Early Archaic Chinese, II, The Word <u>Jo</u>," <u>T'oung Pao</u> XLVII (1959) pp. 281-293.

descriptive statement, etc., are all part of an integral
and consistent whole. This study is only understandable
in the terms in which its predecessors were made.

(iii) Late Han Literary Chinese

      "Late Han Literary Chinese" (= Late Han) like its
predecessors, "Early Archaic Chinese," "Middle Archaic
Chinese" and "Late Archaic Chinese," is an analyst's
abstraction. It is, in fact, the "idiolect" of one
writer of the Late Han period and in particular the
language he uses when translating Archaic Chinese into
a simple literary form of Chinese current in his day.
He also uses, for didactic purposes and in a quite
separate context, a highly contrived "classical" style,
which I have called "Late Han Classical Chinese." The
latter draws deliberately on archaic forms and usages
while the former, as deliberately, avoids archaic usage.
When therefore mention is made in this study of "Late
Han," it must be understood in this accommodated sense.
It is in fact Late Han usage as represented by one author
in one text that has been scientifically analysed.
Similarly, a number of grammatical features have been
described as "Late Han innovations." This again must be
understood in an accommodated sense. They are innovations as far as Archaic Chinese is concerned, but they
may well have antedated our Late Han author.[11]

      The "sample" is a paraphrase with extended comment-
ary on a text of some 35,226 words. It must contain
something like a 100,000 words. The extent to which it
is typical of other Late Han authors is yet to be determined, but most of its innovations (as notes scattered

----

[11] See postscript.

throughout this book indicate[12]) are common to such Late
Han writers as Jenq Shyuan (鄭玄) (127-200 A.D.), Wei
Jau (韋昭) (204-273 A.D.), Gaw Yeow (高誘) (2nd Cent.
A.D.) and Wang Yih (王逸) (fl. 2nd Cent. A.D.) when
writing in similar vein.[13] But, when writing in Late Han
Classical Chinese, our author uses a style, vocabulary
and grammatical forms very similar to those of the Han
writer Ban Guh (班固) (39-92 A.D.). Details in the
description of "Late Han Literary Chinese" and of "Late

----

[12] See 2.2.i footnote; 3.1.v Note; 3.2.i Note;
3.5.i Note; 4.3.i Note; 5.4.iii Note; 5.5.i Note; and
5.5.ii.

----

[13] Examples cited from the works of these Late Han
writers have been culled from the critical apparatus of
Jiau Shyun (焦循) in his Menq-tzyy jenq-yih (孟子正
義 .) A.H.C. Ward has made a detailed study of the
Commentary (注) of Gaw Yeou (高誘) on the Leu-shyh
Chuen-chiou (呂氏春秋). He has kindly supplied
the following examples from Gaw Yeou, in addition to
those cited in Jiau Shyun's Commentary. 人 > 他人 (cf.
2.3.iv); 勿 > 無 (cf. 3.1.i); 特 > 但 (cf. 3.2.iv); 于 > 於
(cf. 3.4.v); 自 > 從 (cf. 3.5.i); 奚自 > 何從 (cf. 3.5.i);
由 > 從 (cf. 3.5.ii) 無或 > 無有 (cf. 4.2.i); 咸 > 皆 (cf.
4.2.ii); 孰 > 誰 (cf. 4.2.iv); 緻 > 邪 (cf. 5.4.i); 選間
and 少選 > 須臾 (cf. 5.5.ii); 選間 is glossed as 猶選
頃也 and 間 in 居有間 as 頃 (cf. 5.5.ii); 安 > 異 (cf.
5.5.ii); 猶 > 尚 (cf. 7.3.iii); 若 > 汝 and 而 > 汝 (cf.
8.1.i); 惡 > 安, 惡用 > 安用 and 奚 > 何 (cf.8.3.iv); both
愈 and 彌 > 益 (cf. 9.1.); 茲 > 此 (cf. App. II). He also
notes: as agential distributive 畢 > 盡; as noun 始 > 初;
as verb 以 > 用 and 殆 > 必; 幾 "nearly" > 近 and 微 "if it
were not for" > 無 .

Han Classical Chinese" may need modification in the light
of further researches, but as an interim stage, the
assumption that the sample is typical is a useful one,
since it enables us to plot the main outlines of evolutionary change from Archaic to Han.

The sample of Late Han Literary Chinese is taken
from the Menq-tzyy Jang jiuh 孟子章句 of Jaw Chyi 趙岐
(d. 201 A.D.). The Jang-jiuh consists of Chapter
Summaries - - the Jang-jyy 章指 - - and of a Commentary
- - the Juh 注 - - upon the text of Mencius. Jaw Chyi
has arranged the text into "chapters" jang 章 and divided
the chapters into sentences and paragraphs jiuh 句 .
Hence his title - - Jang-jiuh. The Chapter Summaries
appear at the end of each chapter, and the Commentary is
interspersed between paragraphs and sentences.

The language used by Jaw Chyi for the Commentary is
quite different from the language used for the Chapter
Summaries. The Commentary consists largely of paraphrase. Jaw Chyi says in his Preface[14] that the Commentary was prepared for those "beginning their studies."
The language of Mencius was already five hundred years
old in Jaw Chyi's time. Its archaisms would occasion a
beginner difficulty. His purpose in using paraphrase
was expository and the language he uses for exposition
is clearly the sort of "easy wen-yan" that those
"beginning their studies" in the Late Han period would
understand. The paraphrase is, in short, translation
from Late Archaic Chinese into Late Han Literary Chinese.
The Chapter Summaries, on the other hand, are homiletical
in character. They are written in a highly contrived and

---

[14] See Menq-tzyy Tyi-tsyr (孟子題辭) (page 24)
in Menq-tzyy Jenq-yih, for details of which see para.
iv below.

lapidary style. They use the four-stress line, and are
replete with archaic usages drawn indifferently from the
Classics of all periods of Archaic Chinese.[15] The
Commentary, by contrast, studiously avoids archaic
usages as being incompatible with its avowed purpose and
keeps to contemporary forms.

For the purposes previously mentioned the language
of the Commentary is characterized as "Late Han Literary
Chinese," and the language of the Chapter Summaries as
"Late Han Classical Chinese," since the language of the
latter is deliberately imitative of the language of the
Classics, while the former, as deliberately, avoids
classical usage because it is its aim to explain such
usage.[16]

(iv) Method and Statement

As already mentioned above, this study is a further
stage in a long-term programme of research. It makes
certain procedural assumptions, is conducted by certain
analytical procedures, and follows a consistent pattern
in descriptive statement. For a description and discussion of them the reader is referred to the Introduct-
ions to Late Archaic Chinese and to Early Archaic Chinese.

-----

[15] A listing is given in Appendix II.

-----

[16] Yoshikawa Kōjirō says "It is logical to suppose
that the modes of expression which later appeared in
the New Anecdotes were already flourishing in the
colloquial of Later Han times, but if so, Pan Ku
admitted none of them whatsoever" ("SHIH-SHUO HSIN-YÜ
and Six Dynasties Prose Style" translated by Glen Baxter
HJAS 18 (1955), pp. 124-141). Most of the features

Systems of romanization and conventional signs and
abbreviations follow the pattern standardized in the
above-mentioned works. References in this work to the
"Text" refer to the text of Mencius as published in the
Menq-tzyy Jenq-yih, 孟子正義 of Jiau Shyun 焦循 (1763-
1820). References to the "Commentary" 注 are to the
Commentary of Jaw Chyi, as it appears in the Jenq-yih.
Pagination for examples is given by section (tseh 冊)
and page number of the edition of the Jenq-yih published
in the 國學基本叢書簡篇 (Basic Sinological Series
(Shorter Collection)). A page reference followed by the
character 章 refers to the Chapter Summaries 章指 appear-
ing at the end of each chapter in the Jenq-yih.
(v) Method and Procedure

In the present study the language of the Commentary
has been analysed according to the procedures described
in Late Archaic Chinese. The resulting description was
then compared with the description of Mencius as given
in LAC. In that comparison certain forms in the Text
were seen consistently to be replaced in the Commentary,
while others were, as consistently, retained, and

Yoshikawa describes (俱 "both"; 欲 "potential"; 寧可
"interrogative"; 耶 "final"; 相 and 復 in parasitic usage;
and 是 "copula") are present in Jaw Chyi and thus were,
as he supposes, current in Han times. Features described by Yoshikawa not attested by Jaw Chyi are 輒 "for
his part" (Jaw Chyi uses 輒 "each time"); 便 "and" (Jaw
Chyi uses 便 "at once"); and the intensive negatives 定不
and 都不 which do not occur in the Commentary at all.
Whether such features were "colloquial" or not is a
matter on which most linguists would hesitate to hazard
an opinion. I have supposed them to be prima facie
features of a simple literary style.

further, it was observed that the <u>Commentary</u> had forms
and usages unknown in the language of the <u>Text</u>. These
features were then abstracted. They constitute a catalogue of (i) features of Late Archaic Chinese still
current in Late Han; (ii) features of Late Archaic
Chinese obsolescent in Late Han; and (iii) innovations of
usage in Late Han. Such a catalogue provides a measure
of the nature and extent of evolutionary change in the
five hundred years that elapse between the language of
the <u>Text</u> and that of its paraphrase.

Description in this book takes the form of a report
on the differences, level by level, and element by
element, between LAC and Late Han. Description is devel-
oped in the hierarchical order followed in <u>LAC</u>. Taken
together, these individual differences form a consistent
pattern. This pattern, which has been characterized as
the "Archaic-Han Shift," is summarized in Chapter 10.
<u>Mencius</u> quotes extensively from the <u>Shu Jing</u> (書 經)
and the <u>Shy Jing</u> (詩 經). Jaw Chyi paraphrases these
citations. In Appendix I the differences between EAC
and Late Han as it is revealed in these paraphrases are
described. The differences reflect precisely the same
tendencies as a comparison of LAC and Late Han reveal.
Mention has already been made of the difference in
language between Late Han Literary Chinese and Late Han
Classical Chinese as shewn by Jaw Chyi's use of the
latter for homiletical purposes. An analysis of this
"Late Han Classical Chinese" is given in Appendix II.
Finally, many of the features of the "Archaic-Han Shift"
foreshadow the emergence of features of Modern Standard
Chinese. The most suggestive of these are summarized in
Appendix III. Finally, Jaw Chyi in his <u>Commentary</u> has a
number of observations of a philological nature. From
these something can be deduced about Chinese ideas on

language in the 2nd Century A.D.   These are described
in Appendix IV.

(vi) The Archaic-Han Shift

A comparison of the contrastive features of Early,
Middle and Late Archaic Chinese has shewn that almost
the entire repertory of grammatical auxiliaries under-
goes change between the 11th and the 3rd Centuries B.C.
But while this is so, EAC, MAC and LAC retain common
characteristics.   The main burden of grammatical indication lies with the "empty words."   The "full words"
keep largely to single forms and enjoy a wide measure of
syntactical ambivalence.

A comparison of the contrastive features of LAC and
Late Han, on the other hand, shews a radical and fundamental shift.   It is not merely, as with Archaic Chinese,
that individual forms evolve and change, but that a
fundamental shift takes place in the respective roles of
the "empty" and "full words."   The Archaic-Han Shift is
away from the precise, predictable and major role of the
"empty words" of Archaic Chinese in making grammatical
distinctions towards the use of periphrastic means for
making these distinctions in Late Han.   The consequent
loss in both role and meaning of the "empty words" is
accompanied by greater complexity in the "full words."
The trend is towards compound rather than single forms
and to greater restriction in syntactical deployment,
so that the degree of ambivalence between nounal,
adjectival, verbal and adverbal usage of the "full words"
of Archaic Chinese is greatly reduced by Late Han.   The
"full words" in their compounded forms tend to be deployed either as nouns or as verbs - and not to
permutate.

Evolutionary change, as it occurs throughout Archaic
Chinese, is a change in _form_ but not in _role_ for the

"empty words." But, as the language passes through the
Archaic-Han Shift, the <u>role</u> of the "empty words" as a
class is changed. The role of grammatical indication
passes to some extent to the "full words" in their new
and more complex forms.

Quite clearly in the critical five hundred years
from LAC to Late Han a change of the greatest importance
in the historical evolution of the language takes place.
We might say that the characterization of the grammatical
auxiliaries of Chinese as "empty words" in Archaic Chinese is a misnomer, but, once the Archaic-Han Shift takes
place, the characterization becomes appropriate. Many
of the changes of the Archaic-Han Shift are towards
features familiar in Modern Standard Chinese. The
"Archaic-Han Shift" therefore marks a critical stage in
the path of evolutionary progress in the language. At
this critical stage the language reaches, as it were, a
fork in the road. One literary form of the language
(Late Han Literary Chinese) is contemporary, keeps
abreast of change, and moves perceptibly towards Modern
Chinese. Another form (Late Han Classical Chinese) is
conservative, deliberately retaining, under the influence
of canonical authority, archaic forms and features. But
both forms, literary and classical, in some degree reflect contemporary change. Late Han Classical Chinese
is not a pure imitation of Archaic Chinese. It is a form
in which archaic features give an antique effect. Late
Han Literary Chinese avoids these archaisms. But both
forms, Literary and Classical, betray themselves by certain innovations typical of the period as Late Han lang-
uages.

LATE HAN CHINESE

CHAPTER 1

T H E   A R C H A I C   H A N   S H I F T

Jaw Chyi's paraphrase of Mencius provides the historian
of the grammar of the Chinese language with a most valuable source of information. Placed side by side with
the text of <u>Mencius</u>, it is an almost perfect index of
evolutionary change in the language from the 3rd Century
B.C. to the 2nd Century A.D.

In the chapters which follow these changes are described, level by level, and element by element. In
Chapter 2 changes at the syntagmatic level, in Chapters
3-6 changes at the sentential level and in Chapter 7
changes at the intersentential level are described. In
Chapters 8 and 9 changes that occur in substitution and
certain other features, best treated by an inter-level
approach, are also described. At the end of each chapter
a summary of change is given. In their totality these
changes can be described more generally and this is done
in Chapter 10.

CHAPTER 2

S Y N T A G M A

In syntagma, or word-group formation, the principal
changes in Late Han from LAC usage are: (i) the blurring
of the distinction made in LAC between the determinative
forms and the pregnant forms of the pronouns and demonstratives (see 2.1-2.3); (ii) shifts between pronominal
and demonstrative usage (see 2.3.ii-iv); (iii) semantic
change in a collective and the introduction of a new
restrictive (see 2.4); (iv) another role for the particle
of syntagma jee 者 (see 2.5); and (iv) blunting in the use
of the particle of determination jy 之 (see 2.6).

2.1. The Personal Pronouns

i. Obsolescence of Determinative Forms

In LAC a distinction is made in the personal pronouns
between determinative and pregnant usage. In the first
person the determinative form is wu 吾 and the pregnant
form is woo 我 . In the second person the determinative
form is eel 爾 and the pregnant form is ruu 汝 (see LAC
2.6.4.1). Wu, woo, and eel occur in Late Han in the determinative role, with that role marked by the particle
of determination jy 之 . This collocation of pronoun plus
determinative particle (吾之;我之;爾之 etc.) is unknown to LAC. Wu and eel have clearly lost their distinctively determinative role (see also section 4.1.i
below, where the determinative pronouns lose their agent-
ive role also).

Examples
敬吾之老亦敬人之老愛我之幼亦愛人之
幼 "We should respect our own aged and too

respect the aged of others. We should love our own
young ones and too love the young ones of others."
(1.58)

Text 吾浩然之氣 "my greater physical vigour"
becomes 我之所有浩然之大氣也 "the greater
physical vigour which I have" (2.61); compare also
我之教命 "my instructions" (2.9); 我之愆 "my
fault" (3.37) 我之功 "my merit" (5.83) 於我之身
"in my person" (5.73); 夫射遠而至爾努力也
其中的者爾之巧也 "to attain distance when
shooting with a bow is a matter of your physical
strength, but to score a bull's eye is a matter of
your skill." (6.7)

Note. Jaw Chyi often paraphrases direct speech as
indirectly reported speech. The pronouns of direct
address therefore occur less frequently in the Commentary
than in the Text. This makes it difficult to collect an
adequate sample of the use of the personal pronouns. For
example, in 6.74 the Text reads 曰吾弟則愛之秦人
之弟則不愛也，是以我為悅者也故謂之內 "[Kao
Tzu] said 'I feel love for my younger brother, but I feel
no love for the younger brother of a man of Ch'in. And
so, because [my brother] provokes a feeling of pleasure
within me, I therefore say it [love] is internal.'" This
in paraphrase becomes 告子曰愛從己則己心悅，故
謂之內 "Kao Tzu said that love proceeded from himself
and so his own heart felt pleasure. Therefore he called
[love] internal." Of some 30 determinative usages of wu
in the Text, for example, only two are paraphrased in
direct speech.

2.2. The Anaphoric Pronouns

i. The Blunting of Distinctions

In LAC, the anaphoric pronouns (chyi 其 in the deter-

minative form and <u>jy</u>之 in the pregnant form) are strictly
differentiated (see <u>LAC</u> 3.8). In Late Han, this differentiation is occasionally blurred.[1] <u>Jy</u> occurs where, in
LAC, <u>chyi</u> would occur.

　　<u>Examples</u>
　　<u>Text</u>: 勿視其魏魏然
　　<u>Commentary</u>: 勿敢視之魏魏 "disregard their awe-
someness" (8.100); in the <u>Commentary</u> 當本之志 is
in parallel with 不可 ... 害其辭 "you should take
for your basis [of interpretation] <u>its</u> [<u>i.e.</u> the
poem's] intention ... you cannot ... do violence to
<u>its</u> phrasing" (5.101); 故民從之教化輕易也
"Therefore the people follow his teaching with ease"
(1.68); <u>Ju</u>諸 is used in Late Han for <u>jy</u>之 (see 5.3.ii
below). In the following <u>chyi</u> not <u>jy</u> would be LAC
usage.[2] 比諸見放也 "by the time that he was ex-
iled" (5.93); 禦人,以兵禦人而奪之貨 "a high-
wayman is one who detains people by force of arms and
takes away <u>their</u> property" (6.28).

2.3. <u>The Demonstratives</u>
　　i. Obsolescence of Determinative Forms
　　Although, in LAC, the demonstrative <u>tsyy</u>此 is used
determinatively (for example此極 "these extremities" as

―――――――
[1]The blunted use of <u>chyi</u> in other Han authors has
been noted by Leu Shwu-shiang 呂叔湘. See <u>Hann-yeu</u>
<u>yeu-fa</u> <u>Luen-wen Jyi</u> 漢語語法論文集(Peking 1955),
p. 181.

―――――――
　　[2]For examples of "<u>bih chyi</u> verb" (比其彡) see
W.A.C.H. Dobson "Towards a Historical Treatment of the
Grammar of Archaic Chinese - - Early Archaic <u>Yüeh</u> >
Late Archaic <u>Chi</u>," HJAS 23 (1961), pp.5-6.

in 1.77), the form restricted to determination is <u>sy</u> 斯
(see <u>LAC</u> 2.6.4.2). In Late Han, <u>sy</u> is replaced by <u>tsyy</u>.
This suggests that forms of the demonstrative restricted
to the determinative role are obsolescent in Late Han.
(<u>Sy</u> as a conditional conjunction in LAC is also obsolescent in Late Han and is replaced by <u>tzer</u>則; see 7.2.iv
below.)

Examples
斯 is replaced by此 in 4.86; 1.34; 1.109; 5.119 (將
for斯 in some editions is a misprint).

The two demonstratives of Late Han <u>tsyy</u>此 and <u>shyh</u>是
both occur in determinative usage, sporadically, with the
particle of determination <u>jy</u> 之.

Examples
<u>Tsyy jy</u> occurs in如此之用 "usages of this kind"
(7.50). <u>Shyh jy</u> occurs in 於是之際 "in these extremities" (7.101 (章)).

ii. <u>Chyi</u> as a Demonstrative
An innovation in Late Han is the extended use of the
determinative anaphoric pronoun <u>chyi</u> as a demonstrative
before certain nouns. In this usage, <u>chyi</u> bears a resemblance to the Modern Standard Chinese <u>jehgeh</u> and <u>jeh-</u>
<u>yanqde</u> (這個 and 這 樣的), for example, <u>chyi</u> might be
translated <u>jehyanqde</u> in 眾皆悅美之,其人自以所行
為是而無仁義之實   "The crowd all like and
admire him. This sort of person thinks his own course of
conduct is right, but he lacks the reality of Humanity
and Justice."(8.117)   And in the following example <u>chyi</u>
might be translated <u>jehgeh</u>. 我不絜其人之行,故不教
誨之,其人感此,退自修學而為仁義,是亦我教
誨之一道也 "I do not think this person's conduct
is pure and so I do not teach him. But such a man will

be affected by this, and, retiring from my presence, cultivate learning on his own and so become Humane and Just.
This,too, is one way for me to teach him." (7.66)

Examples

Other examples of chyi as a demonstrative are 而其人
"yet such a man" (7.85);其國君臣 "the princes and
ministers of these states" (8.67);喜其人 "pleased
that this man's ..." (7.54);得其人舉之 "obtained
such a man and promoted him" (7.59);其井田之大要
"The essential points of this well-field system"
(3.82). See also 1.53.

iii. Chyi in Chyi-shyr etc.
Chyi also occurs before shyr 實 in chyi-shyr 其實 "The
fact of the matter is ...," "In reality ...," and in chyi-
jong 其終, "In the end ...," "finally ..."

Examples
其實但為合眾之行 "In reality, this is merely
conforming with the crowd" (8.115);是以其終亦
皆弒其君 "So that, in the end, all of them assass-
inated their princes" (1.10). See also 5.62 (章).

iv. Chyi before Ren
In LAC ren 人 "man" often occurs in a pronominal usage
in the sense of "other than the person speaking or the
person addressed, others, etc," as for example, 則人將
曰 "then others will say" (7.55). In the translation of
this passage into Late Han, it is rendered 則其人將曰
"then others [= chyi-ren] will say" and the passage continues 訑訑賤他人之言 "How smug he is! He regards
what others say with contempt" (7.56). Here both chyi-
ren and ta-ren occur for "other men." Before this pronominal ren both chyi and ta are synonymous. Chyi in the
sense of "other, the rest" also occurs in chyi-yu 其餘 .

Examples

Late Han uses <u>ta-ren</u> for pronominal <u>ren</u> in 8.7;
6.126; etc. Other nouns determined by <u>ta</u> are 他 國
"another State" (7.30); 他 辭 "some other excuse"
(6.27); 他 事 "other things" (2.3); 他 故 "some other
reason" (5.10). <u>Chyi-yu</u> occurs in 此 二 者 猶 天 下
之 父 也 其 餘 皆 天 下 之 子 耳 "These two elderly
statesmen were, as it were, the fathers of the
Empire, the rest being all the Empire's children"
(4.103); and determinatively in 其 餘 指 "the other
fingers" (6.116).
Thus, <u>chyi</u>, a pronoun in LAC, becomes, in Late Han (a)
confused with its pregnant form <u>jy</u>, (b) extended in usage
as a demonstrative "this, this sort of" and (c) from a
contrastive form with <u>ta</u> (<u>chyi</u> "this," <u>ta</u> "the other")
becomes assimilated with <u>ta</u> as "other." <u>Chyi</u> in this
latter usage has an echo in the modern <u>chyitade</u> 其 他 的
"the other, others."

   <u>Note</u>.It is difficult not to suspect an historical
connection between the LAC demonstrative <u>sy</u> 斯, its re-
pression in Late Han times, and the occurrence in Late
Han of a <u>chyi</u> 其 demonstrative. Again the occasional 其 -
之 confusion in Late Han, and the occurrence of <u>chyi</u> as
a demonstrative, recall the use of <u>jy</u> 之 as a determinative demonstrative in LAC, which is peculiar to <u>Juang-
tzyy</u> (as for example in 之 蟲 "these insects") and <u>Leu-
shyh Chuen-chiou</u> (as, for example, 之 子 "such a person's
children," and 之 二 國 者 "these two states," <u>LSCC</u> VI.5
and XVI.3, <u>Syh-buh Bey-yaw</u> Ed.) but which also occurs in
this sense on the Oracle Bones. (See <u>LAC</u> 6.4.6.2 footnote 18.)

2.4. <u>Collectives and Restrictives</u>
   i. Shift in meaning of <u>Farn</u>
   <u>Farn</u> 凡 , which occurs in LAC as a collective before

nuns in the sense of "all" or before numbers as "the sum
total of" (see LAC 2.6.4.5), occurs in Late Han in the
ex ended sense of "all, > commonplace, > ordinary, common." In LAC it is purely collective. Farn min "all of
the common people" does occur in Mencius (7.83), and it
is perhaps from such contexts that the shift to "every-
day, commonplace" occurs. The shift does not seem to
have taken place until Han times. An example from the
Commentary is 譬若和氏之璧雖與凡主之璧尺寸厚
薄適等,其賈豈可同哉. "By way of illustration, the pi
of the Ho Family, though of comparable size and thickness
with an ordinary jade pi, could hardly be thought equal
in value!" (3.116.)

Examples
凡人 "ordinary person" occurs in 5.127 in contrast
to 聖人 "sage"; in 6.114 in contrast to 君子 "the
princely man"; and in 4.21, 5.66, 6.112, 7.66 (章),
etc. 庸人 "ordinary people" occurs in 7.33 (章) and
iong compounds with farn in 凡庸之君 "rulers of the
ordinary sort" in 7.66. 凡品 "[people of] the ordinary
sort" occurs in 8.69 in contrast to 大聖 "great sages"
and 凡夫 "ordinary men" in 7.77. Farn occurs as a
noun in 卓絶乎凡 "far removed from the common run
[of men]" in 7.85 (章).

ii. Dann before Nouns
An innovation in Late Han is the introduction of the
restrictive dann 但. Dann has a wide range of distribution (see Aspect section 3.2.iv and v, Polarity section
3.6.ii, Copula section 6.1.ii and Conjunction section
7.1.ii). In syntagma it occurs before nouns in the sense
of "only, only a."

Examples
徒善 "mere goodness" in <u>Mencius</u> is rendered in the
<u>Commentary</u> 但有善心 "merely to have a good heart"
(4.73), but in 但重累之數皆翼之飾有異 "only
the number of layers, and the decoration of the cof-
fin, were different" (3.4), <u>dann</u> occurs before nouns.

2.5. The Particle of Syntagma

i. <u>Jee</u> as a marker of Cause

In Late Han, <u>jee</u> 者, in addition to its syntagmatic
function, becomes a marker of causal clauses. Thus,
"verbal clause/<u>jee</u>" becomes "the reason why ..."

Examples
美之者欲以責之也 "The reason why he addressed
him in this formally elegant fashion, was because he
intended thereby to administer a rebuke" (8.116).
The clause of cause is also introduced by <u>suoo-yii</u>,
thus, 孔子所以危於陳蔡之間者其國君臣
皆惡 "The reason why Confucius ran into difficulties
in Ch'en and Ts'ai was because the princes and ministers of those states were evil" (8.67); other examples
occur in 5.57 (twice); 4.36 (twice); 3.22; 2.16;
1.103, etc.

2.6. The Particle of Determination

i. Blunting of usage

In LAC, the determinative relationship between two
nouns is marked by <u>jy</u> 之 when the relationship is one of
membership in a class, or of possession (see <u>LAC</u> 2.62)
Attributive determination is unmarked. In Late Han <u>jy</u>
occasionally occurs between attribute and noun.

Examples
聖之人 "a Sage" (5.24); 污亂之世 "a depraved and
disorderly generation" (8.117); 寶重之器 "valuable

vessels" (2.18); 密細之網 "a fine net" (1.24); 先
聖之王 "the former Sage Kings" (1.94). 不賢之人
"an unworthy man" (1.14); 不正之道 "an improper
way" (7.78).   Other examples are in 2.106 (章),
2.40, 1.67, 3.108, 6.49, 3.116, etc.

<u>Note</u>. For other changes in the use of <u>jy</u> 之 in Late
Han see 2.1.i, 2.2.i above, and 5.3.i and ii, and 8.1.i
and ii below.

2.7   SYNTAGMA IN SUMMARY

LAC	LATE HAN	
	Changes in usage	Innovations in usage
2.1 吾：我 > 　　爾：汝 >	我：我之[吾] 爾：爾之[汝]	
2.2 其：之	Occasionally blunted	
2.3 斯：此 >	此／是：with possible 此之： 是之 (斯 also be- comes 則) 其 demonstrative: 其 "other"	
2.4 凡 "all" >	凡 "common"	但 "only a"
2.5 者 (syntagma)	者 (syntagma) 者 (causal)	
2.6 之 generic 　　only	之 generic and attributive	

In syntagma, therefore, the principal shift is away
from specialized determinative forms towards the use of
_iy_ 之 as an all-purpose determinative particle, following
both nouns and attributes, pronouns and demonstratives.

This leads to the obsolescence of certain of the specialized forms of the pronouns and demonstratives of LAC
and to semantic shifts, blunted usage, and reduction of
role of others. This shift away from specialized forms,
towards all-purpose general forms, is a characteristic
generally of the Archaic-Han shift, and will be illustrated further later.

CHAPTER 3

T H E   V E R B

The principal changes in Late Han from LAC usage as they
concern the verb are:

(i) A reduction in the role played by the negatives
before verbs in determining mood; blunting in the use of
the modal negatives; the emergence of bu 不 and wu 無 as
all-purpose negatives and their restriction in role to
negation; the increase in the use of periphrasis to indicate modality and the introduction of new periphrastic
modal forms (See 3.1.)

(ii) Important shifts in role and meaning of certain
aspectuals and the occurrence of new aspectuals (See 3.2.)

(iii) The resuscitation of the EAC post-verbal particle tzay 在 (See 3.4.v.)

(iv) A reduction in the role of the post-verbal particles in determining voice, with an increase in the resources for, and the use of periphrastic means of indicating voice (See 3.4.)

(v) Obsolescence of certain polar forms and the
introduction of a new one (See 3.6.)

3.1. Mood

i. The reduction of the role of the Modal
   Negatives to negation

The negatives in LAC play the chief role in determining the mood of the verb (see LAC 3.3.1). They disting-
uish between the indicative (不) and non-indicative moods
(injunctive 毋 subjunctive 無). Two of these modal negatives have a stressed form (indicative 弗 and injunctive
勿), and the indicative has also a form (未) which
denies experience of, rather than instances of an act.

In Late Han the tendency is towards indicating modality in the verb by periphrastic means and for the negatives to be restricted in function to negation only. This
is shown by (i), a tendency to replace the negatives of
LAC with bu 不 -- Bu thus becomes a general-purpose negative without modal connotation; and (ii), a tendency to
create negated modal forms by using bu in compound forms.

Examples

Examples of LAC negatives replaced with bu:

LAC 弗 is replaced by 不 in 8.27, 8.90; 6.114, 6.125,
7.8, 5.13, 4.125, 6.112, 2.22.[1]

LAC 未 is replaced by 不 in 3.48, 3.110, 2.8.

LAC 無 is replaced by 不 in 3.79, 1.27, 1.107, 3.7.

LAC 否 is replaced by 不 in 5.123, 5.110.

LAC 勿 is replaced by 不 in 1.15, 2.56.

LAC 非 is replaced by 不 in 1.72, 6.77.

Examples of bu 不 in negated compound modal forms are
不須 6.28; 不當 2.90, 2.55; 不得 2.82, 5.10 etc.

Note. Yeou 有 "to occur, or to have," however, is negated with wu 無 . Wu ceases to have modal connotations
here and has simply the role of "negation before yeou."
Examples are 無復有 "will no longer have" (7.77); Wey-
yeou 未有 occurs in the Commentary as in the Text in
2.81, 2.82, but is rendered wu-yu 無有 in 2.82 and wu 無
in 1.71 and 1.11; Wu-yu "There was not" occurs in 2.51,
1.113, 1.100.

---

[1] Fwu 弗 is consistently replaced by bu 不 in the
Commentary (20 occurrences), except where it is re-
placed by bu deei 不得 (1.98 (twice) and 8.40) and by
bu-keen 不肯 (6.112); Fwu occurs once only in the
Commentary (4.97). It is clearly obsolescent in Late
Han.

ii. The blunting of the Modal Negatives

One consequence of the reduction of the grammatical
role of the negatives is the occurrence of the modal negatives of LAC in blunted and imprecise usage.

<u>Examples</u>

勿 is used for LAC 無 in 7.37.

勿 is used for LAC 不 in 4.83 (章).

莫 is used for LAC 無 in 5.116 (章); 5.80 (章).

莫 is used for LAC 不 in 6.115; 6.117 (章).

未 is used for LAC 不 in 5.20; 6.117 (章); 7.22;
7.26; 7.17; (章); 1.94.

無 is used for LAC 非 in 3.39 (章).[2]

Another consequence is that the modal negatives of
LAC are expanded to make clear their modality.

<u>Examples</u>

無 becomes 無可 in 8.117 and 不得 in 2.22; 7.37

勿 becomes 不可以 in 1.28, 不可 in 2.29, and 可無
in 1.106.

iii. Stressed or Intensive Negatives are
replaced by periphrastic forms

Stressing and intensification of the negatives, for
which special forms are used in LAC (see LAC 3.3.1.1 and
2), tends, in Late Han, to be achieved by periphrastic
means. LAC has <u>jong-bu</u> 終不 but Late Han introduces
<u>jinq-bu</u> 竟不 ; <u>bih-bu</u> 必不 ; and <u>shu-wu</u> 殊無 in sense of
"absolutely not, never on any account, certainly not" etc.

———————

[2] It will be seen that most examples of the blunted
use of LAC negatives occur in the <u>Chapter Summaries</u>
where their use is intended to give an archaic effect.
This is typical of Late Han Classical Chinese. See
Appendix II.

Examples

今竟不能有燕 "Now, he never could possess Yen" (3.14); 必不受之 "He would on no account accept it" (bih-bu here replaces fwu 弗 in the Text) (8.18); 殊無所問 "there was absolutely nothing to ask about" (1.48).

iv. Modification in meaning of Wey

While the negative wey 未 which denies experience of, rather than instances of an act in LAC (see LAC 3.3.1.1) occurs in Late Han, it is sometimes replaced by bu 不 (for examples see section 3.1.i above). It occurs typically in Late Han in the narrower sense of "not yet, not so far," and, in this sense, also occurs before numerals.

Examples

未成人 "not yet attained manhood" (4.26); 上世未制禮之時 "in past generations at a time when the Rites had not yet been formulated" (3.122); 未來仕齊也 "not yet come to be employed in Ch'i" - i.e. "before he was employed in Ch'i"(3.20); 己仁恩之未至 "His own imperfect realization of Humanity and kindness" (lit: Humanity/kindness's/not-yet/perfect) (2.104); 孺子未有知小子也 "Ru-tzyy 'baby' is a child before it is aware of things" (lit: not-yet-have knowledge) (2.96); 未葬 (lit: "not-yet buried") > "prior to the burial" (3.55); 未四十 "not yet forty" (2.50).

Note 1. In the last two examples wey is used, as bu-iyi 不及 or bih 比 are used in LAC.[3] 未及 occurs in 未及解稅祭之冕而行 "He left, (even) before he had removed his sacrificial cap" (7.30) but in the Chapter Summary this becomes 冕不及稅 (7.33 (章)).

---

[3] See footnote 2.2.i.

Note 2. The reduction in the roles of the negatives
in Late Han, and the blurring of the distinctions made by
the modal negatives of LAC, are also accompanied by the
obsolescence of an LAC feature, whereby polarity is expressed by shifting substitutes (pronouns and demonstratives) from the post-verbal to the pre-verbal position
when negated, for which see section 3.6.i below.

   v. The blunting of the modal role of Guoo
      and Guh

In LAC, mood in the verb when unnegated is unmarked.
When, however, a change of mood takes place, the zero in
zero/verb may be replaced by positive replacements. In
the indicative, the positive replacements are guh 固 and
guoo 果 (see LAC 3.3.1.4).

   In Late Han this purely modal function of guh and guoo
is lost, leading to the replacement of gu by suh 素 "as of
old" (an innovation in Late Han), and by charng 常 "as
always," and to the glossing of guoo by neng 能 "able to"
and you jinq 猶竟 "like jinq ('in the end')." Guh and
Guoo are then used in these non-modal senses.

   Examples
   Guh is replaced by 常 in 3.119.
   Guh is replaced by 素 in 2.17.
   Suh "habitual, habitually, as formerly, formerly,"
   occurs in 5.86; 6.67; 4.24 (章); 7.60.
   Guh "really" 3.37; 3.21 (before noun); 2.122.
   Guh is used for "as of old, habitually" in 8.54.
   Guh is used for "former, formerly," in 4.2.
   Guoo is glossed by neng "able to" in 5.66; 5.17;
   2.33; 2.122.
   Guoo is glossed by you jinq, "rather like saying 'in
   the end'" in 6.77.

Guoo is used in 果毅 guoo-yih "of fixed purpose" in
2.128.

Note. 固 故 古 seem quite unstable in Late Han. Guh
故 "therefore" is used for 古 "old" in 故舊 "old friends"
(8.111; 8.38) and in 舊 故 for "ancient" in 舊 故 文章
"ancient documents" (4.73). In 2.3 the gloss 故者舊也
occurs. Guh 固 is used for guh 故 "therefore" in 4.107
(章) and in military usage for "strongpoint, defences"
in 2.113 and 2.116. This may explain why Jaw Chyi often
reads modal guh as suh "habitually, as of old," and as
charng "as always." Guoo being glossed as neng 能 "able
to" may result from some resemblance between guoo 果 and
EAC keh "able to" (Karlgren *Klwâr and *K'ək). (See the
Jeng-yih s.v. in 2.33 where Jiau Shyun notes that the
Late Han scholar Wei Jau reads 果克也).

vi.   The replacement of Yeou and Wei
      in the Subjunctive

The positive replacements for the subjunctive mood
in LAC are 有 for 無 and 為 for 不為   (See LAC 3.3.1.3).
Late Han tends to avoid these altogether. A curious replacement for modal yeou "should, ought" is the word guey
貴 "noble" used putatively and injunctively "should give
honour to," as for example in 君 子 有 不 戰, 戰 必 勝 矣
"a gentleman should not fight, but if he fights, then inevitably he wins" which is translated 君 子 之 道, 貴 不
戰 耳; "In the code of gentlemen it is thought honourable not to fight" (2.116), but which the Ch'ing scholar,
Jiau Shyun (loc. cit.) renders 有 不 戰 不 當 戰 也.
This same replacement occurs in 朋 友 有 信 "friends
should trust [each other]" which is translated as 朋 友
貴 信 "friends should regard with honour the trust they
have in each other" (3.104).

Examples

<u>Guey</u> occurs in parallel with <u>bih</u> in 人必趨命貴受
其正 "Man must pursue his fated course, and should
honourably accept his proper fate" (7.73 (章));
compare also 貴令後世可繼續而行耳 ﹕ "[The
prince] should [so rule] as to make possible the con-
tinuance of his works by his descendants" (2.24)
(<u>Text</u> here has 為可繼也); and 學尚虛己師誨
貴平. "In learning [a prince] must humble himself.
When the teacher instructs, he should be treated as
an equal" (8.38 (章)). Conversely, <u>yeou</u>有 is used
for <u>guey</u> in 自有獻子之家 "though they honoured
the House of Hsien-tzu" (6.21).

<u>Note</u>. For Ancient Chinese, Karlgren reconstructs 為
*jwie,貴 *kjwei,有 *jiəu.

vii. The marking of the Injunctive

The positive replacements for the injunctive and
hortatory negatives in LAC are <u>dang</u>當 and <u>deei</u>得 (see
<u>LAC</u> 3.3.1.4). Both occur in Late Han, but <u>dang</u> occurs
with such markedly increased frequency that it is possible that by Late Han the injunctive mood is marked,
whether a change of mood takes place or not. <u>Dang</u> and
<u>deei</u> are negated with <u>bu</u>.

Examples
(a) <u>Dang</u> occurs in the <u>Commentary</u> where mood is unmarked in the <u>Text</u>. 4.22, 2.134, 2.120, 2.122,
2.116, 2.104, 2.90 (twice), 1.104, 3.86, 3.63, 3.92,
8.103 etc.
(b) <u>Dang</u> is negated with <u>bu</u> 2.90, 2.55, 2.68 etc.
(c) <u>Deei</u> is negated with <u>bu</u> 1.24 (twice), 2.8 (章),
2.82, 5.10.

Note 1. In LAC shang 尚 occurs in an injunctive sense
in Tzuoo Juann (see LAC 3.3.1.2). Shang occurs in the
Chapter Summaries in 學尚虛己 "in learning one should
humble oneself" (8.38) (but on this see Appendix 2).
Shang-dang occurs in the Commentary, however, in 尚當
問王道 "and so he should have asked about the Way of
True Kingship" (1.48).

Note 2. Dang also occurs as a verb "assume responsibility for, take office as, be equal to or adequate for"
etc. Examples are 自謂能當名世之子 "he himself
said [or thought that] he could fulfil the role of a
"scholar famous in his generation" (3.37); 猶當王者
"Even so, one who has assumed the responsibility of Kingship ..." (3.12); 何爲當勸齊伐燕乎 "Why would I
have assumed the authority to advocate that Ch'i should
attack Yen?" (3.12); see also section 7.2.iv below.

viii. The use of Shiu and Ing
Late Han has injunctive and hortatory modals unknown
to LAC. One occurring with high frequency is shiu 須
"ought, should." It is negated with bu.

Examples
Shiu occurs before the verb in an injunctive sense
in 4.72; 4.112; 4.19; 4.89 (章); etc. Shiu occurs
as verb in sense of "should have or be" in 8.66 (章);
7.84; 4.74; 4.79 (章); 4.80; 4.65; 5.81. Shiu is
intensified by bih 必 in bih-shiu "must have or be" in
4.64; 2.10; 3.13 (章); 4.84 (章); Shiu is negated
with bu in 6.28.
Ing 應 "to reply," "to match up with" has, in part,
semantic affinities with dang 當 "to match up to, to
correspond to." Ing also occurs, as does dang in an injunctive sense.

Examples

是應得其理也 "and so one must get its principle right" (8.54 (章)); 應法而去 "must go forth in accordance with the laws" (1.97). 虛則不應 "If the reality is lacking, then it does not match up" (8.28章).

Note 1. Bih 必 occurs before verbs in Late Han in the sense of "decidedly, inevitably, of a certainty" etc., for example 必亡 "will certainly be lost" (4.77); 必醉 "will assuredly become drunk" (4.82); 必欲行其道 "will inevitably want to put his way into practice" (2.108) etc. Bih is negated with wey in 未必同也 "is not necessarily the same" (7.26), with bu in 不必知 "did not necessarily know ..." (3.17), and 不必留此學也 "did not need to stay here, to study" (7.11), and with 非 in 庸言必信, 非必欲以正行為名也性不忍欺人也 "his every word can certainly be relied upon, not necessarily because he wants to gain a good reputation thereby, but because, by nature, he cannot bear to deceive others" (8.99). Bih occurs before bu (for which see section 3.1.iii above). Bih intensifies shiu 須 in sense of "must have a, must be a" (see 4.64; 2.10; 3.13章), and combines with dang in 當必造朝也 "must certainly go to Court" (2.120). Bih is itself injunctive in 國必修政君必行仁 "the State must cultivate good government, the prince must practice Humanity" (2.89章); see also 1.91 (章), 1.96; etc.

Note 2. Yi 宜 "proper", is used putatively and in hortatory sense "should properly" "properly speaking" and thus, like guey 貴 (see 3.1.vi), has an injunctive and hortatory function. It occurs in 君命宜敬當必造朝 "a prince's summons should be respected, you must certainly go to Court" (2.120). 宜無以錯於廉恥之心 "There should not be that which runs counter to the con-

scientious heart" (7.78). In this sense dictionaries
equate <u>yi</u> with <u>dang</u> 當 and <u>ing</u> 應 (see <u>Tsyr Hae</u> s.v. <u>dang</u>
and <u>yi</u>).

    ix. The modal functions of <u>Kee</u> and <u>Neng</u>

    <u>Dang</u>, <u>deei</u>, <u>shiu</u>, and <u>ing</u> in their negated forms and
<u>kee</u> "permitted to, might, could, can" and <u>neng</u> "able to,
can" in a negated form tend to replace the injunctive
negatives of LAC, or to supplement them, while the positive form takes a double negative, viz. <u>bu kee bu</u> 不可不
and <u>bu neng bu</u> 不能不.

3.2. <u>Aspect</u>
    i. Shifts in Potential and Momentary Aspect
    Some important functional and semantic shifts occur
in the aspectual determinations of the verb in Late Han.
LAC <u>chiee</u> 且, potential aspect, "about to" shifts in Late
Han to momentary aspect, "for the time being" or "at this
moment." LAC <u>yuh</u> 欲 desiderative aspect, "wish to" shifts
in Late Han to potential aspect, "about to" "going to."

    <u>Examples</u>
<u>Gu</u> 姑 "for the time being" is glossed by <u>chiee</u> 且 in
2.9 and 2.76. <u>Chiee</u> "for time being" occurs in 且
使輕之 "let me lighten [taxes] for the time being"
(4.39); in 且宿留 "so I stayed for the time being"
(3.38); and see also 8.30. <u>Chiee</u> "at that or this
moment" occurs in 2.88. <u>Chiee</u> "for a moment" occurs
in 且坐 "sit down for a moment" (3.29). <u>Chiee</u> also
occurs in the older sense of "about to" in 6.30; and
compounded as <u>chiee-yuh</u> 且欲 for "about to" in 3.119.
<u>Yuh</u> occurs as potential in 欲如何說之 "How are
you going to remonstrate with them?" (7.19) and in
欲絕 "about to break off" (8.73) - see also 3.27;
將欲 occurs in 1.61 for potential aspect.

Fang 方 momentary aspect "at that or this moment" occurs in Late Han in 5.62 and 5.87, which, with chiee, gives fang-chiee 方且 "at this moment," "just on the point of," in 3.29. Jann 暫, momentary aspect, "for the time being," occurs as an innovation in Late Han, re- placing jah 乍 "this/that moment" in 2.96, and occurs also in 2.111.

Note. In Han times, yi-chieh is used in the sense of "momentary" as in 以徼一切之勝 "in order to seize a momentary advantage" (How Hann Shu, Wang Bor Juann) or, "interim or emergency" as in 一切增賦 "an interim in- crease in taxes" (Hann Shu, Dyi Fang-Jinn Juann). Yi- chieh occurs in the Commentary in this sense in 取為一 切可勝敵 "They seek for possible momentary advantages over the enemy" (7.78). (This meaning is very well dis- cussed by Jiau Shyun in the Jenq-yih, loc. cit.)   In Modern Standard Chinese yi-chieh means "entirely, the whole." It would be of interest to know when the shift of yi-chieh, "momentary" > "the entire, the whole" takes place.

ii. Perfective Aspect

For perfective aspect LAC has jih 既 and yii 已. Late Han prefers yii, replacing jih in the Text by yii. Jih occurs in Late Han in a different usage, in which yii does not occur (for which see section 5.1.ii below).

Examples

Jih is glossed by yii 既已也 (2.139) and replaces jih in 8.62 (2 occurrences); 1.22 etc. Yii occurs in 已下 "already descended" (5.82); 已正 "already rectified" (4.83); 已見 "already appeared in" (4.83); 已美 "already splendid" (7.85); 已說 "already ex- plained" (8.51); 已盛 "already flourishing" (1.43); 已足 "adequate already" (2.46); 已定 "already settled" (2.49.)

iii. The use of <u>Fuh</u> for Durative and
   Iterative Aspect

An important aspectual shift introduces an innovation in Late Han - <u>fuh</u>復. <u>Fuh</u> frequently replaces
<u>yow</u>又 not only in its aspectual function "once again"
(see <u>LAC</u> 3.3.2.8.a), but also as a conjunction "and too"
(for which see section 7.1.i below·). But <u>fuh</u> also occurs
in Late Han for durative aspect and functions like LAC
<u>you</u> (猶) (see <u>LAC</u> 3.3.2.4). <u>Fuh</u> occurs with such high
frequency in Late Han, occasionally parasitically, that
it might be considered peculiarly characteristic of Late
Han. Yoshikawa Kōjirō observes that, later, in Six
Dynasties' usage, <u>fuh</u> has "almost no significance."[4]

   In its aspectual role, <u>fuh</u> occurs both negated and
unnegated, marking durative or continuative aspect.
Negated it occurs in sense of "not any longer," "not any
further," "not any more." Unnegated it occurs in sense
of "continue to, still." <u>Fuh</u> also occurs marking iterative aspect as in LAC in the sense of "once again,
again," often in contexts where English has a verb with
the prefix re-, as for example 欲復搏之 "intending to
recapture it" (8.76).

Examples
(a) Durative Aspect, negated. 不復食羊棗 "he did
not eat dates any more" (8.105); 不復為路 "no
longer a road" (8.70); 心欲去,故不復受祿 "but
in his heart he wanted to leave, and so did not
accept a salary any more" (3.38). See also 6.8; 6.47;
4.116; 8.79.
(b) Durative Aspect, not negated. 豈可復謂之外也
"it surely cannot be, that it can still be said to be

---

[4] Yoshikawa Kōjirō "SHIH-SHUO HSIN-YÜ and Six
Dynasties Prose Style", <u>HJAS</u> 18 (1955), p. 131.

external" (6.79); 豈可復殘傷其形體 "it surely cannot be, that he can continue to do harm to his body?" (6.64); 富貴而復有德 "rich and highly placed yet still possessed of virtue" (6.21); see also 6.57; 6.47; 3.43; 1.19; etc.

(c) Iterative Aspect

復貢之 "offered him again" (7.25); 復往求見 "went again seeking an interview" (Text has 又) (3.119); 復行古法 "put into practice again the ancient ways" (1.107). See also 5.114; 7.77; 8.76; 8.79; 3.115; 3.124; etc.

(d) Fuh occurs as a verb in, for example, 4.39 "revive" and in 3.77 "restore"; as "anew, newly" in 新復 (3.70); and as "a further" before numerals as in 復 三年 "after a further three years" (3.111). Fuh, however, appears to be tautologous and hence parasitic in 復申 "to repeat" (1.12; 1.19; 1.59 etc.) and in 復歸 which is not "to return again" but merely "to return" (8.1).

iv. Dann and Aspect

A further important innovation of Late Han is the introduction of the restrictive dann 但． It is of very frequent occurrence, and, like fuh, might be considered in its frequency to be peculiarly characteristic of Late Han. Determining the verb in the aspectual position, dann occurs as "merely, only," and is comparable with dan 單 in LAC.

Examples

凡人但不能演用為行耳 "the ordinary person merely cannot apply them in practice" (2.97); 但有 爵耳 "He merely possesses a noble title" (2.123); 但治其爭訟 "only settled their disputes" (3.25); 人君但養犬羸 "Rulers merely provide food for

their dogs and pigs" (1.30); 水豈無分於上下乎，
水性但欲下耳，"It surely cannot be that water
cannot differentiate between upwards and downwards!
Water, by nature, merely wishes to flow downwards!"
(6.66). 不但坐而聽命 "He does not merely sit
awaiting the dictates of fate" (8.79). Other examples
will be found in 7.24; 7.45; 7.27; 7.8; 6.24; 6.44;
etc.

v. <u>Dann</u> and Polarity

    But <u>dann</u> is of such frequent occurrence in Late
Han, and the restrictive aspect of comparatively rare
occurrence in LAC, that it is difficult to dismiss all
occurrences of <u>dann</u> before verbs as purely aspectual.
<u>Dann</u> is often in comparable distribution with <u>bu</u> 不, as,
for example, 但言 ... 不言 ... "he merely said ... he did
not say ..." (2.74); 但聞 ... 不聞 ... "I have only heard
that ... I have not heard that ... " (2.8); 但加載書
不復歃血 "He merely attached the document [to the
sacrifice] but did not, also, smear the blood on the lips
[of those swearing the oath]" (7.37); 但食之而不愛
... merely to feed him but not to love him ..." (8.27);
人君但崇庖廚養犬馬不恤民 "Princes merely de-
vote their attention to their kitchens and to the care
of their horses and hounds, but they do not shew compass-
ion for the common people" (4.50); 不勸王使我得行
道，而但勸我留 "You did not advocate that the King
should allow me to put my Way into practice, but merely
advocated that I should be detained" (3.30). Other examples will be found in 8.27; 2.92; 2.125; etc.
    Here, <u>dann</u> is functioning in a way reminiscent of
<u>wei</u> 惟 in its polarity with <u>fei</u> 非 in EAC (see <u>EAC</u> 4.8).
Looked at from the point of view of its polarity with <u>bu</u>,
<u>dann</u> might be thought of as of a class with the negatives,

as a sort of partial or restricted negation. <u>Dann</u> here,
as it were, anticipates a total negation. Whether expressed (with a <u>bu</u> clause) or not, <u>dann</u> involves an antithesis.

    Unnegated <u>dann</u> anticipates a negative antithesis.
Negated, as for example in 不但坐而聽命 "He does not
merely sit awaiting the dictates of fate" (8.79), <u>dann</u>
anticipates a positive antithesis. In this instance it
is supplied in the context. 聖人亹亹不倦, 不但坐
而聽命故曰君子不謂命也 "The Sage is indefatig-
able, never tiring. He does not merely sit awaiting the
dictates of fate. That is why it is said 'the True
Gentleman [i.e. Confucius] did not discuss fate.' In all
the pre-verbal occurrences of <u>dann</u> there is, either dir-
ectly expressed with a conjunction (<u>erl</u>) or implicit, an
adversative.

    <u>Note</u>. <u>Dann</u> in Late Han is thus not far removed from
the adversative conjunction <u>dann-shyh</u> 但是 "but" or <u>dann-
tzer</u> 但則] of Modern Standard Chinese, and may possibly,
in Late Han, have occurred in this conjunctive sense, as
the following examples suggest: 之以為當同其恩愛
無有差次等級相殊也. 但施愛之事, 先從己親
屬始耳. 若此何為獨非墨道也 "Chih thought that
we should shew love and kindness to all equally - that
there should not be any discrimination between the degrees of kinship and of rank. But, in the matter of
shewing love, that we should begin with our own kinsfolk.
If this was so, [Chih thought] why should the Mohists be
singled out for censure?" (3.120); and, in his paraphrase
of <u>Songs</u> 192 cited in 1.109, Jaw Chyi has 居今之世可
矣, 富人. 但憐憫此黨獨羸弱者耳 "Living in this
present age, it is the rich who get by, but pity these,
the weak and lonely" (1.109).

    These examples are not conclusive, for the first may

well be 但施愛之事 . "It is only in the matter of
shewing our love that we ..." and the second be "I merely
pity these, the weak and lonely." In all the fifty-three
occurrences of dann in the Text, these are the only two
examples that might even be thought of as conjunctive.

vi. The use of Jyi and Biann

Jyi 即 which occurs in LAC as a copula (see LAC
4.4.2) and as a conditional conjunction (see LAC 5.3),
occurs in the aspectual position in Late Han in the sense
of "at once, immediately." This usage is an innovation
in Late Han.

Examples
不欲即去 "I did not want to leave immediately"
(3.38); 知攘之惡當即止 "If you know stealing
them to be wrong, you should stop doing it at once"
(4.40); 所止舍館未定,故不即来 "The arrange-
ments for the lodgings at which I was to stay were
not yet settled and so I did not come at once"
(4.122); 舜入而即去,瞽瞍不知其已出 ...
"Shun went down into [the well] but came out immediately afterwards. Ku-sou, unaware that he had already come out ..." (5.82). Jaw Chyi's use of jyi
leads him to translate 即不忍其觳觫 "It was true
that I could not bear to see its shuddering" as 即
見其牛哀之 "As soon as I saw that ox, I pitied
it" (1.53), thus retaining jyi in his translation but
giving it a Late Han meaning.

In similar usage, biann 便 occurs in Late Han as an
innovation, seemingly interchangeably with jyi. It
occurs in the sense of "at once, immediately, straight-
away."

Examples

公何為不便見孟軻 "Why did your grace not see
Mencius straight away?" (2.31) (Jiau Shyun, in his
Jenq-yih in loc., says "便 is like 利,利 is like 快.
The passage means 其遲滯不即見 "He dallied, not
seeing him at once.") 彼不復問孰可,便自往伐
之 "They did not also ask me 'who should [attack
Yen]' but, of their own volition, immediately went
off and attacked it" (3.12); 陽貨視孔子亡而饋之
者,欲使孔子來答,恐其便答拜使人也 "The
reason why Yang Huo sent a gift of food when he saw
that Confucius was not at home was because he wished
to make Confucius come to him to return the visit.
He was afraid that [if Confucius were at home] he
would immediately bow to the messenger [and thus fulfil his obligation to return the visit]" (4.36).

vii. The use of Meei and Jer

In LAC meei 每 occurs before the verb in the sense of
"on each occasion, each time" (see LAC 3.3.2.8). In Late
Han, che 輒,an innovation, fulfils this role, either
singly or in combination with meei, viz. meei-jer 每輒.

Examples

丑怪孟子不肯每輒應諸侯之聘不見之於
義謂何也 "[Kung-sun] Ch'ou was perplexed at
Mencius' unwillingness to reply each time to the
invitations of the Feudal Lords [and asked] what
principle of justice was involved in his not seeing
them" (4.34); 不知可繼續而常來致之乎,將
當輒更以君命將之也 "I do not know if he can,
time after time, be continually coming and presenting
gifts, or if he should bring them, having obtained
the prince's order afresh each time?" (6.43); 每人
而輒欲自加恩以悦其意,則日力不足以足

之 也 "If each time he wishes to be kind to each and
every man that comes in order to please the dictates
of his desires, then his daily strength will be insufficient to satisfy their needs" (5.8); 過 小 耳
而孝子感激, 輒怨其親, 是亦不孝也 "When
the faults of the parents are minor ones but the
filial son is moved to anger by them, so that each
time (they happen) he feels resentment against his
parents, then this, too, is to be unfilial" (7.15).

3.3. Manner

i. The misinterpretation of Yan

The Commentary twice interprets "verb/yan 焉" as an
attribute (either reading yan for ran 然, or as a maw
貌).[5] x-yan, and xx-yan, thus, by Late Han times, are
interpreted as x-ran or xx-ran. (See also Section
5.3.ii below.)

Examples

Text 心有戚戚焉   "in my mind, there was a sense
of familiarity with it (i.e. with what you said").
Commentary 戚戚然, 心有動也 "chi-chi-ran means
as when the mind is stirred" (1.55); Text 眸子眊焉
"The pupil of the eye is dulled by it"; Commentary
眊者蒙蒙目不明之貌 "Mau means 'as though
blindfold, the eye not seeing'" (4.108). Neither
occurrence gives a materially false interpretation
of the Text but yan is given the value ran and not
of yu jy, as, properly, it should be given in
Mencius.

---

[5] For maw see Appendix 4.

ii. The interpretation of '<u>yeou/attribute</u>'
    and '<u>attribute/sy</u>'

The occurrence of <u>attribute/sy</u> 斯, and <u>yeou</u> 有 /
<u>attribute</u> in the <u>Book of Songs</u> is commonly interpreted
by Han writers as a reduplication of the attribute.[6]
This influences Jaw Chyi's interpretation of <u>Mencius</u>.

<u>Examples</u>
<u>Text</u> 其顙有泚 "His brow broke out in sweat" but the
<u>Commentary</u> explains (no doubt influenced by a gloss
on 有泚 in the <u>Songs</u> as 鮮明貌, see <u>Jenq-yih</u> <u>in loc.</u>)
as 泚 汗出 泚 泚然也 "<u>tzyy</u> means "glistening with
sweat" (3.123). But, on a citation from the <u>Songs</u> in
the <u>Text</u>, 王赫斯怒 "The King flushed in anger," the
<u>Commentary</u> has 王赫然斯怒 (1.88).

3.4. <u>Voice</u>

In LAC, the voice of the verb is governed by the
disposition of the two post-verbal elements (see LAC
3.4). The positions vis-à-vis each other of these two
elements is governed by their relation to the particle
of the post-verbal position (in LAC 於 and 乎 and in EAC
于). While, in LAC, these particles do not always occur
with predictable regularity, their function, in so far as
the voice of the verb is concerned, is decisive. In Late
Han there is a perceptible shift towards indicating voice

---

[6] See Wang Shean 王顯 "Shy-jing jong gen chorng-yan
tzuoh-yonq shiang-dang-de Yeou-tzyy shyh, Chyi-tzyy
shyh, Sy-tzyy shyh, her Sy-tzyy shyh." 詩經中跟重言
作用相當的有字式,其字式,斯字式,合思字式
<u>Yeu-yan Yan-jiou</u> 語言研究 4 (1959), pp. 9-43.

by periphrastic means and for the post-verbal particles
to become simply markers of the locative.

i. The <u>Jiann</u> Passive

The use of <u>jiann</u>見 for the periphrastic passive is
of rare occurrence in LAC. In Late Han it is exceedingly
common. In addition Late Han introduces three innovations for marking the passive voice, namely, <u>wei</u> 為 ;
<u>bey</u>被 ; and <u>meng</u> 蒙 .

<u>Examples</u>

In the <u>jiann</u> passive, <u>jiann</u> occurs immediately before
the verb. <u>Jiann</u> occurs twice and <u>wei</u> once in the
following translation of an LAC original which has
no passive voice at all. 言為人所悅 將見禪為
天子皆不足以解憂獨見愛於父母為可以
解己之憂 "It means, delighted in by others and
about to be placed in the succession for the Throne -
neither of these two things was sufficient to dispel
his [Shun's] grief. Being loved by his parents, by
that alone could he have dispelled his grief" (5.77).
The positional passive of the <u>Text</u> is replaced by the
periphrastic passive in 不 悅 於魯衛 which becomes
不見悅魯衛之君 "disliked by the rulers of Lu
and Wei" (5.125), and an unmarked passive is replaced
by the periphrastic passive in 以貨取乎 which becomes 以貨財見取乎 "[When has a True Gentleman
been] procured with a bribe?" (2.128). Other examples are 見愛 "beloved" (8.116);見薄 "shabbily
treated" (8.39);見惡 "hated" (5.72);見放 "exiled"
(5.93);見稱 "designated" (5.127);不見用 "unem-
ployed" (6.34);見削奪 "be encroached upon" (7.26);
見貢 "be offered up" (7.25);見亡 "be destroyed"
(4.89);不見知 "be unknown" (5.70);見侮慢 "be

treated with discourtesy" (4.92);見 浸 "be invaded"
(2.88) etc.

ii. The Bey Passive

A metaphorical extension of the verb bey 被 "to wear,
to cover" and thus > "to be under the effect of" > "be
affected by," "to suffer," produces, when occurring before another verb, a periphrastic passive.

Examples

Bey "to wear," "be clothed by" occurs in 則天下被
覆衣之仁也 , "then the world will be clothed in
the covering-cloak of Humanity" [literally "covering-
cloak-Humanity"] (4.74). (The Text puts this in the
active voice 仁覆天下   "Humanity covers over the
world.") "Affected by" occurs in 使百姓被澤 "so
as to allow the people to be affected by its refresh-
ing dews [i.e. its beneficence]" (4.72). See also
被恩 "affected by kindness" (8.45 (章)); Bey
occurs as "suffer" as in 被病 "suffering from sickness" (6.87) and 被其害 "suffer harm" (8.44). But
in the following bey, almost devoid of semantic con-
tent, merely marks the passive 常常被服 "forever
controlled (by it)" (8.71 (章)).

Note. Meng 蒙 "to receive, meet with, etc." is comparable to bey in 被其害 "suffer harm" (8.44) in a proverb
cited in the Commentary 鳶鵲蒙害仁鳥曾逝 "When
kites and magpies suffer harm the kindly [?edible] birds
fly high" (5.12); Meng also occurs in 蒙其恥辱 "be
regarded with contempt by them" (2.85).

iii. The Periphrastic Passive in _Wei_

In the distribution "<u>wei</u> 為/active agent/<u>suoo</u> 所/ verb" the verb is passive, but the "<u>wei</u> α <u>suoo</u> β" matrix itself is a syntagma and occurs only as a unit in sentences.

<u>Examples</u>

(a) wei   X   Y

不 為 俗 移 "not shifted by fashion" (7.84) (章)

(b) wei   X suoo Y

為 知 者 所 笑 "laughed at by those who know" (8.76); 為 眾 口 所 訕 "reviled by everyone" (8.67); 為 楚 所 滅 "destroyed by Ch'u" (5.125); 為 曾 西 所 羞 "despised by Tseng Hsi" (2.48) (章).

(c) Examples of positional passive in the <u>Text</u> translated in the <u>Commentary</u> by the <u>wei</u> passive. <u>Text</u>: 而 薉 於 物 <u>Commentary</u>: 為 物 所 薉 "and so are impinged upon by objects" (6.122); <u>Text</u>: 終 身 不 養 為 <u>Commentary</u>: 終 身 不 為 妻 子 所 養 也 "for the rest of his life he was not looked after by his wife and children" (5.61).

<u>Note</u>. The <u>jiann</u>, <u>wei</u> and <u>bey</u> passive forms occur, each in a distinctive form of distribution. This is best shown in tabular form.

<u>Pre-verbal</u>	<u>Verb</u>	<u>Post-verbal</u>
Either 以 [<u>noun</u>]	見 /<u>verb</u>	[or <u>noun</u>]
	被 [<u>noun</u>]	[or <u>verb</u>]
為 [<u>noun</u>]	所 /verb	

The <u>noun</u> in parenthesis is in each case the instrumentality through which the agent suffers the action of the verb, and, as will be seen, is in contrastive distribution in all three forms of the periphrastic passive. In the case of <u>jiann</u> this instrumentality occurs postverbally in 不 見 悅 魯 衛 之 君... "disliked by the rulers of Lu and Wei" (5.125) and pre-verbally in the

instrumental position in 以貨財見取乎 "procured
with a bribe!" (2.128).   In the case of <u>bey</u> the instrumentality occurs immediately after <u>bey</u> as in 亦并被
其害 "and both are harmed by it" (8.44), where <u>chyi hay</u>
is nominal, "suffered its harmfulness," but in examples
like 被服 "controlled by it" (8.71), <u>bey</u> occurs before a
verb.   (A not dissimilar possibility occurs in Modern
Standard Chinese, viz. 欺他 <u>chi-ta</u> "cheat him" 他被欺
了 <u>ta bey chi-le</u> "he was cheated," 被了他的欺 <u>bey-le</u>
<u>ta-de chi</u> "cheated by him!")   In the case of <u>wei</u>, <u>wei</u>
introduces the instrumentality, and <u>suoo</u> (when occurring)
marks the verb.

    iv. Causative and permissive
    The periphrastic causative in LAC is formed with
<u>shyy</u> 使 (see <u>LAC</u> 3.4.5).   Late Han uses <u>shyy</u> but also
introduces <u>linq</u> 令 , which is interchangeable with <u>shyy</u>.
The periphrastic causative is of much more frequent
occurrence in Late Han.   <u>Shyy</u> and <u>linq</u> also occur in Late
Han in an extended sense, from "cause, bring about, make"
to "permit, let, allow."

    <u>Examples</u>
    Examples of the permissive use of <u>shyy</u> and <u>linq</u> 皆
不欲使世子行三年 "None of them wanted to allow
the Heir Apparent to serve the three year mourning
period" (3.49); 且無令土親肌膚 "further, not to
let the earth come into close contact with the body"
(3.7).
    <u>Note</u>. <u>Ting</u> "to listen, to obey" occurs in Late Han in
an extended sense, as "to let or to allow."   Examples
are 文王聽民往取禽獸 "King Wen allowed his people
to go into [his park] and take game" (1.82). 告則不聽
其娶 "if he had told them, they would not have allowed

him to marry" (5.81). 說 以 方 且 聽 子 為 政 "they
explained that [the King] was just about to allow the
Master [i.e. Tzu-ssu] to take charge of the government"
(3.29).

v. Tzay as a post-verbal particle

The particles of the post-verbal position of LAC are
yu 於 and hu 乎 (see LAC 3.4) and of EAC, yu 于 (see EAC
3.4). Hu 乎 and yu 于 are obsolescent in Late Han and are
replaced by yu 於. Yu 於, however, is occasionally replaced by tzay 在 or occurs in combination with tzay, i.e.
tzay-yu 在 於.[7] The tendency in Late Han is for these
particles to become simply markers of the locative and
for their role in the indication of voice in LAC to be
supplanted by the periphrastic means already described.
Yu 於 occurring in the Text is sometimes disregarded altogether in the Commentary.

Examples
於 is replaced by tzay-yu in 2.99;
乎 is replaced by yu in 4.85, 8.117, 5.25;
乎 is replaced by tzay in 4.108;
於 is replaced by tzay in 4.32, 6.125;
在 is used for yu in 2.65, 5.21, 3.47, 8.120, 2.82.
Yu in the Text is disregarded in 入 於 井 which becomes 入 井 (2.96); 害 於 天 下 which becomes 害 之
(2.61); 擇 於 斯 二 者 which becomes 擇 此 二 者
(2.29); 快 於 是 which becomes 快 是 (1.61); 造 於
朝 which becomes 造 朝 (2.120.) See also 3.122, where

---

[7] 在 in 在 於 in LAC is a verb. It occurs as "verb/
post-verbal particle," "to reside in, to lie with, etc."
In Late Han 在 於 occurs in the collocation "verb/tzay-yu/
post-verbal element" and is thus a particle of the post-
verbal position.

諸 (=之於) is disregarded in the <u>Text</u> in 有諸內
必形諸外 which becomes 有中則見外 "what one
possesses inwardly is manifested outwardly" (7.27).

<u>Note</u>. <u>Tzay</u>, in this usage, is not an innovation in
Late Han, but the resuscitation of an EAC feature in
Late Han (see <u>EAC</u> 3.4.5.1 especially footnote 26). For
other resuscitations see sections 4.2.v and 5.1.ii below.

3.5. <u>Direction</u>

i. <u>Tzyh</u> is replaced by <u>Tsorng</u>

When direction is treated periphrastically, LAC <u>tzyh</u>
自 "from" is consistently replaced in Late Han by <u>tsorng</u>
從 . <u>Tzyh</u> in Late Han usage is used, singly or in combination, for "self" (as reflexive when in the pre-verbal
position, and in the agential distributive position in
sense of "agent acts in his own interests, or in person"
- usually contrary to expectation"). <u>Tzyh</u> is also used
in Late Han in a new sense as a form of concession (see
section 7.3.i below). This suggests a sort of chiasmus.

LAC   LATE HAN
<u>Tzyh</u> 自 "from"   <u>Tsorng</u> 從 "from"
<u>Tzonq</u> 縱 "even if"   <u>Tzyh</u> 自 "even if"

<u>Examples</u>
<u>Tzyh</u> is defined as <u>tsorng</u> in 5.110 and 3.73, and
<u>tsorng</u> replaces <u>tzyh</u> in 3.4, 3.43, etc. <u>Tzonq</u> occurs
as a verb in Late Han, in the sense of "to loosen,
let go" (6.87 and 6.105) and as an attribute in
"loose living" in 4.25.

<u>Note</u>. The replacement of <u>tzyh</u> "from" by <u>tsorng</u> "from,"
in Late Han writers, is remarked on by Jiau Shyun who
observes that other Late Han scholars, Jenq Shyuan 鄭玄
(127-200 A.D.) in his <u>Notes</u> 箋 on the <u>Book of Songs</u>, and
Gau Yow 高誘 (2nd century A.D.) in his <u>Commentaries</u>
on the 呂氏春秋 and on the 淮南子 "both take <u>tzyh</u> to
be <u>tsorng</u>" (皆以自為從) (<u>Jenq-yih</u> 3.74).

ii. You is replaced by Tsorng

LAC also uses you 由 for the periphrastic treatment
of direction. You, like tzyh (see para. i above), is
consistently replaced by tsorng 從 and thus is obsolescent
in this sense in Late Han.

Examples

You is replaced by tsorng in 2.40, 2.81, 3.120, 6.87,
and by yu 於 in 4.42.

Note. You 由 also occurs in LAC used for you 猶 "is
like." The Commentary has two occurrences of you in this
usage (2.67 and 2.68) but elsewhere replaces you with ru
如 , ruoh 若 or pih-you 譬 由 (1.44, 2.39, 6.7). You before a verb is modal (as is you 猶) in LAC. This is disregarded in translation (see section 3.1.vi above). The
verbal usage of you "to use, to avail oneself of, to pursue [a course] or follow [a road]" occurs indifferently
in LAC and Late Han. Late Han, however, uses her-you 何
由 , not in the sense of "from whence" as in LAC, but in
a new sense of "of what use." (See section 8.3.v below.)
You is twice defined as 用 也 (5.70, 7.76) and this is its
main use in Late Han.

3.6. Polarity
    i. The obsolescence of the polar form
       'negative/substitute/verb'

LAC has a feature in which a negated verb, particularly when the verb is negated with a stressed negative,
drops the pronouns and demonstratives which would occur
in the post-verbal position, if the verb were not negated.
This feature is unknown to Late Han. In translation, the
dropped pronoun is often supplied, and numerous examples
occur of negated verbs followed by pronouns and demon-

stratives. This suggests that between LAC and Late Han a
change takes place in the intonational pattern of the
sentence though this is impossible to demonstrate. It
does, however, provide further evidence of the reduction
in the role of the negatives, already referred to in
section 3.1.i above.

Examples
"不 /verb/pronoun", occurs in 2.73, 3.20, 3.6, 2.139
(章), 2.77, 5.42, 7.8, 6.117, 6.24, 6.27, 4.125,
4.73 (twice), 2.108, 3.119, 2.124, 8.97, 6.112.
"不 /verb/demonstrative", occurs in 1.29, 5.20, 7.55,
1.61.
"弗 /verb/demonstrative", occurs in 4.97.
"無 /verb/pronoun", occurs in 2.20, 4.22, 6.27,
8.115.
"未 /verb/pronoun", occurs in 2.13.
"勿 /verb/pronoun", occurs in 6.112.

ii. Dann and Polarity
A corollary of the dropping of the polar emphasis of
LAC described in the previous paragraph is the occurrence
in paired statements of dann 但 with either a negative or
positive polar statement, explicit or implied. This has
been described already in section 3.2.v above.

3.7.　　　THE VERB IN SUMMARY

LAC	LATE HAN	
	Changes in usage	Innovations in usage
Mood 不：弗　and　未	Tend to converge on 不 and lose modality. 未 becomes "not yet"	竟不；必不；殊無；for emphatic negation
毋　；　勿	> Obsolescent - preference for periphrastic forms	
固　；　果	Lose modality and converge with 能常 etc.	素 "as of old"
有　；　為	Use avoided as modals	
當　；　得	Used with markedly increased frequency.	須；應 "should" "ought" "needs to"
Aspect 且 (potential)	>且 (momentary)	暫；暫且；方且 一切 "momentarily"
欲 (desiderative)	>欲 (potential)	
既；已 (perfective)	>已 (perfective)	
復 (iterative)	>復 (iterative and durative)	

THE VERB IN SUMMARY

LAC	LATE HAN	
	Changes in usage	Innovations in usage
Aspect 單 (restrictive)		但 (restrictive) 但 (in polar role) 但 (adversative)
每 "each time"		輒; 每輒 "each time" 即; 便 "immediately"
Manner	焉 in blunted usage	
Voice 於 (于: 乎) 見 (passive) 使 (causative)	>於; 在; 在於 見 (passive) 為 (passive) 使 (causative and permissive) 令 (causative and permissive)	被 (passive) 蒙 (passive) 聽 (permissive)
Direction 自 "from" 縱 "even if" 由 "from"	>從 "from" >自 "even if" >從 "from"	
Polarity Negative/substitute/verb	Obsolescent	

The principal shift in the verb and its determinations is away from specialized forms of the negative
and towards the use of periphrasis to indicate mood,
which, when in the negative, uses an all-purpose negative, <u>bu</u>. This leads to the obsolescence of certain of
the special modal negative forms of LAC and to the
occurrence of new periphrastic forms to indicate modality. Voice, too, tends towards the use of periphrastic
means, with the consequent reduction in role of the post-
verbal particles, and a tendency away from the strict
positional syntax by which voice is imposed in LAC.

The shift away from specialized forms to the use of
all-purpose forms, is, as has already been seen in the
syntagmatic level (see section 2.7 above), a characteristic of the Archaic-Han Shift. The use of periphrasis
is, too, characteristic with a consequent blunting and
semantic loss among the "empty words," and together these
constitute one of the main features of the Archaic-Han
Shift.

CHAPTER 4

A G E N C Y

The principal changes in Late Han from LAC usage as they concern Agency are:

(i) A preference for the pregnant rather than the determinative forms of the personal pronouns for the Agent (see 4.1).

(ii) The obsolescence of certain specialized agential distributives and the encroachment of <u>jiu</u> 俱 upon <u>jie</u> 皆 and <u>jie</u> 偕 and of <u>shwei</u> 誰 upon <u>shwu</u> 孰. The resuscitation of <u>shyan</u> 咸 (see 4.2).

(iii) The parasitic occurrence of <u>shiang</u> 相 and the obsolescence of <u>jiau</u> 交 for reciprocity (see 4.3).

(iv) Blunted usage in indicating delegated agency (see 4.4).

(v) The restriction of <u>tzyh</u> 自 to the Reflexive (see 4.5).

4.1. The Pronouns

    i. Obsolescence of the agentive forms
      of the Pronouns

    In LAC, where the agent is represented by a personal pronoun, the determinative forms <u>wu</u> 吾 (first person) and <u>eel</u> 爾 (second person) occur. In Late Han these are almost totally replaced by the pregnant forms <u>woo</u> 我 and <u>ruu</u> 汝. This tendency is parallel to the tendency already noted (see section 2.1 above) for the determinative pronouns to become assimilated in the pregnant forms, and for the distinction between the determinative and agential form, on the one hand, and the pregnant form on the other, to disappear.

The determinative pronouns occur sporadically in the Text in the agential position but never in the post-verbal position. If it were not for this, there would be justification for regarding wu and erl in Late Han as simple stylistic variants of woo and ruu.

Late Han still adheres, however, to the "agential/ post-verbal" distinction in the anaphoric pronouns chyi 其 and jy 之 though, as noted in section 2.2 above and elsewhere, blunting and certain semantic shifts occur in the use of the anaphoric pronouns.

Examples

(a) Agential wu is replaced by woo in 1.61, 1.62, 1.66, 1.97, 2.4, 2.134, 3.119, 3.51, 3.52, 3.48, 4.6, 4.51, 6.107, 8.103, etc.

(b) Yu 予 is replaced by woo in 1.18, 2.34, 2.37, 2.127, 2.139, 3.22, 3.33, 4.41, 5.38, 7.66, etc.

4.2. The Distributives

i. The Obsolescence of Huoh 或 and Moh 莫

The agential distributives of LAC -- huoh 或 "of the agents some" and moh 莫 "of the agents none" (for which see LAC 3.5.3.1) -- are obsolete in Late Han as such.

Huoh is consistently paraphrased as yeou 有 or yeou-ren 有人 "there are those who." A possible reason for this is that the function of huoh shifts in Late Han to use as a selective conjunction, in the form huoh ... huoh ... "some ... some ..." > "either ... or ...," developing eventually into a simple selective conjunction "or."

Moh, on the other hand, in common with the other specialized forms of the negatives of LAC, becomes sub-sumed in wu 無 and bu 不 and loses its distinctively agent-ial role.

Examples

(a) <u>Huoh</u> is defined as 有也 in 2.139, and is replaced by 有；有人 etc. in 7.23, 5.128, 5.122, 5.91,
8.90, 5.62, 3.11, 8.30, etc.

(b) <u>Huoh</u> repeated, "either ... or ..." 或殀或壽
"whether they die prematurely, or live to a ripe old
age" (7.70); 或得或否 "whether he gets it or not"
(7.74); 或折或引 "whether by breaking off or
leading forth" (7.67 (章)); 或見或否 "whether he
saw them or not" (7.24 (章)); 或為君子或為小
人 "whether he be a princely man or a petty man"
(6.101).[1]

(c) <u>Moh</u> defined as <u>wu</u>

<u>Moh</u> is glossed by <u>wu</u> 莫無也 in 5.113 and 7.71.

<u>Moh</u> is replaced by <u>wu</u> in 5.100, 3.61, 8.32, 2.121,
        2.102, 3.61, 1.49, etc.

<u>Moh</u> is used like <u>bu</u> in 6.115.

<u>Moh</u> is replaced by <u>chii</u> 豈 in 2.121.

Note. The selective conjunction of LAC is <u>ruoh</u> (see
LAC 2.5). <u>Ruoh</u> 若 occurs in the <u>Commentary</u> in redupli-
cated form, not unlike <u>huoh</u> above. 若遊若豫 豫亦遊
也 "whether it be called <u>you</u> or <u>yuh</u>, <u>yuh</u> is after all
<u>you</u>" (1.96).

---

[1] Janusz Chmielewski in his "Notes on Early Chinese
Logic (II)" <u>Rocznik Orientalistyczny</u> XXVI.2 (1963), pp.
91-106, has an interesting discussion of the evolution
of this usage of <u>huoh</u>. It was not, as he says, listed
in <u>Late Archaic Chinese</u>. This was not an oversight on
my part. The 或 ... 或 ... form does not occur as early
as the Late Archaic period.

ii. The encroachment of <u>Jiu</u> upon <u>Jie</u> and <u>Jie</u>

In LAC, the agential distributive <u>jie</u>皆 "all" and <u>jie</u>偕 "both" are restricted to the agential position (for which see <u>LAC</u> 3.5.3). In Late Han <u>jie</u>偕 is obsolescent and is replaced by <u>jiu</u>俱 . <u>Jie</u>皆 , on the other hand, occurs not only as an agential distributive, but as a collective (an innovation in Late Han), functioning (as does <u>jiu</u>俱) as a determinant <u>via</u> the verb of post-verbal elements; <u>jiu</u>俱 thus subsumes <u>jie</u>偕 , and attracts <u>jie</u> 皆 into the function <u>jiu</u> performs in Late Han. <u>Jiu</u> 俱 also, and wrongly, replaces <u>jiau</u>交 for reciprocity for which see section 4.3.i below.

<u>Examples</u>

(a)俱 replaces 偕 . See 1.18 and 2.111 where 偕 is defined as 俱 ; <u>Jiu</u> occurs in the agential distribut-ive position in sense of "both" in 俱 出 文 王 "both [the T'eng and Lu ducal houses] descended from King Wen" (3.49); 雖 俱 白 "though both are white (6.68); 俱 含 天 氣 "both [men and animals] breathe the air of Heaven" (5.30 (章)). See also 1.23.

(b) <u>Jie</u> as a collective. <u>Jie</u>皆 occurs before the verb, determining its post-verbal elements in 人 不 能 皆 如 其 願 也 "Man cannot do all that he wishes to do" (8.78); 而 皆 信 之 "and believe all of it" (8.49); 能 皆 實 而 無 虛 "[if one] can see as true all of it, and as false none, [then] ..." (7.74); 皆 錄 之 於 春 秋 "recorded them all in the <u>Ch'un Ch'iu</u>" (8.45)舜 ... 皆 取 人 之 善 謀 而 從 之 "Shun accepted all good advice tendered by others and complied with it" (2.106); 孟 子 皆 曰 否 "Mencius replied with a 'no' to all [three questions]" (7.55).

iii. <u>Jiu</u> as a Collective

<u>Jiu</u> occurs before the verb, determining its post-verbal elements in 俱答二人獨見李子 "He replied to both of the two, but saw only one of them namely Chi Tzu" (7.22). 俱有好憎 "has both likes and dislikes" (6.101); 俱賢之 "thought both of them worthy" (5.57).

iv. <u>Shwu</u> is assimilated into <u>Shwei</u>

<u>Shwu</u> 孰 which in LAC usage is restricted to the agential distributive position and is an interrogative substitute ("of the agents which one"?) (see <u>LAC</u> 6.5.2.4) is replaced by <u>shwei</u> 誰 "who"? in Late Han. Where <u>shwu</u> occurs in Late Han, seemingly as a stylistic variant for <u>shwei</u>, it is used in a blunted sense.

Examples

<u>Shwu</u> is replaced by <u>shwei</u> in 8.16, 5.106, 3.12, 3.24, 1.42. Jaw Chyi transposes 膾炙與羊棗孰美 , "Cooked meat or dates - - which of the two is the better [eating]?" to 羊棗孰與膾炙美也 "who thinks dates are better than cooked meats to eat?" (8.105); <u>Shwu</u> is replaced by <u>her-wey</u> in 問二者何為重 "He asked of the two what was the more important" (<u>Text</u> has 禮與食孰重 "The Rites [observed when eating] and eating [itself], which is the more important?" (7.1).)

v. The use of <u>Shyan</u>

<u>Shyan</u> 咸 which occurs commonly in EAC (see <u>EAC</u> 3.5.3) and sporadically in LAC (mainly in citation) occurs in Late Han.

Examples

使無罪者咸恐懼也 "makes all the innocent fearful" (8.39); 咸以仁義相接 "all conducting their inter-relationships according to Humanity and Justice" (7.21); 咸願以為師 "all want to make [them] their teachers" (1.2.)

Note. See also 3.4.v and 5.1.ii for other resuscitations of EAC forms in Late Han.

4.3. Reciprocity
   i. The obsolescence of Jiau and the parasitic
      use of Shiang

In LAC, shiang 相 and jiau 交 (and also the compound form jiau-shiang 交相) occur before the verb to indicate reciprocity of action in the agents.   (See LAC 3.5.4.) Shiang occurs in this role in Late Han, but Jiau is obsolescent. Shiang also occurs, parasitically, before certain verbs, where no reciprocity is intended.

   Examples
   Parasitic shiang: 不相欺愚小 "no cheating of the young and innocent"(3.115); 不相與言 "does not talk to them" (2.139 (章)); 不足以相笑也是人俱走 "They are in no position to laugh at the others, because both groups ran away" (1.23).
   Note. In 1.6 jiau occurs in the Text in the sense of "reciprocity" and is so read by Jiau Shyun (交互之交). Jaw Chyi has as comment 交爭各欲利其身 , and says that another explanation is to read jiau as 俱 . Jiau Shyun observes in this latter connection that both Gau Yow 高誘 in his Commentary on the Jann-gwo Tseh and Wei Jau 韋昭 in his Commentary on the Gwo-yeu read 交 as 俱 . Both are Late Han writers. This suggests that in Late Han jiau for reciprocity is not only obsolescent, but has been wrongly assimilated with the collective 俱 .

4.4. Delegated Agency

i. Wey encroaches upon Wey

Where one agent is said to act for, or in the interests of another, wey 為 introduces the second agent (see LAC 3.5.5). In Late Han wey is occasionally assimilated with wey 謂, particularly in those contexts where wey occurs in yii-wey (以為) constructions. Wey 謂 then occurs, marking "delegated agency."

Examples

(a) 以為 becomes 謂

Text 百姓皆以王為愛也 "The people thought the King was mean" becomes 百姓皆謂王嗇愛其財, "The people thought the King miserly with his wealth" (1.52); Text 於予心猶以為速 "I myself thought that [my departure] was all too fast" becomes 我自謂行速疾矣 , "I myself thought my going very fast" (3.32); 謂孟子欲自比孔子 "thinking that Mencius wished to compare himself with Confucius" (2.74); 小人苟得謂不見知 "petty people gain it by means that are wrong, thinking that it will not be known" (5.70 (章)). Other examples are in 1.53, 3.52, 8.116, etc.

(b) 所以...為 becomes 所以...謂

燕民所以悦喜迎王師者,謂齊救於水火之中耳 "The reason why the people of Yen received the King's armies with such pleasure was simply because Ch'i was saving them from "fire and flood" (i.e. from tyranny)" (2.16).

(c) 為 "do, become, create" becomes 謂

謂窮則獨善其身者也 "If you are impoverished, then cultivate your goodness in solitude" (2.25 (章)). 當謂何也 "What should I do?" (2.19). 謂此詩者 "he who composed this song" Text has 為此詩者 (2.87).

(d) 為 "delegation of agency" becomes 謂
有之於己乃謂人有之　"If you have it in yourself, then have it for others" (8.82).
(e) 謂 in the Text is read as though it were 為
Text: 此之謂 "describes this" but Commentary 是為 不可活也 (2.88).

4.5. The Reflexive

i. The use of Tzyh in compounds

In Late Han as in LAC the reflexive is marked by the occurrence of tzyh 自 before the verb (see LAC 3.5.4.1). Tzyh, however, occurs in certain other forms of distribution, and is then often compounded with gong 躬 , shen 身 "person, body" or jii 己 "self," etc. In the agential distributive position 躬自 ; 躬 ; 自身 ; 身自 and 身 occur, when the agent is performing in person, usually where this is contrary to expectation. In the same position 獨身 occurs in the sense of "agent by himself, alone, to the exclusion of all others." Used with jii "self" jii-tzyh 己自 occurs as Agent. Tzyh also occurs in word-formation for reflexive action in such compounds as tzyh-lih 自利 "self-interest" (1.11); tzyh-shiou 自修 "self-cultivation" (1.93); 自由 "self-from" > "of own volition" (2.134.) Tzyh-ran 自然 "so-of-itself" > "natural," "spontaneous." (2.21, 7.76).

Examples

自 etc. in the agential distributive position
(a) "in person, personally, itself," 兵自殺之 "the weapon itself killed him" (1.31)
不用心於躬自耕也 "not put his mind to ploughing in person" (3.109.) 當身自具其食 "must prepare his food himself" (3.86)
必自身種粟乃食之邪 "must he personally have

grown his food, before he will eat?" (3.87), 自視何
"as you yourself see it, what ...? (3.14);
(b) "alone" 獨自作樂 "play music alone" (1.73).

ii. The use of the Emphatic and Reflexive
    Pronoun Jii
In both LAC and Late Han, the emphatic or reflexive
pronoun is jii 己, "self," which occurs irrespective of
person (referring to the speaker, the person addressed,
and persons other than these), and is deployed indifferently in the agential and post-verbal positions. Jii
also occurs as a determinative in syntagma, often marked
with the particle of determination jy 之. Jii occurs
with tzyh 自 in both jii-tzyh and tzyh-jii. Jii is used
with much greater frequency in Late Han, and is often
preferred in the Commentary where the Text has the non-
reflexive pronouns.

Examples
(a) Jii, Jii-tzyh and Jii-shen in the agential
position
己自狂曲何能正人 "When a man is himself crook-
ed, how can he straighten others?" (4.8). 己所不
欲勿施於人 "do not do to others those things you
do not wish for yourself" (7.94 (章)). 非己身所
能傳 "This is not something which one oneself can
contrive" (2.29).
(b) Jii in the post-verbal position 識仁義之生
於己也 "Realizing that Humanity and Justice are
born within ourselves" (5.30). 非禮招己則不往
"if summoned by an improper Rite, he would not go"
(4.2). 恐其污己也 "fearing that he would defile
him" (2.107).

(c) <u>Jii</u> in syntagma

己之恥 "his own shame" (6.39) 己之賢才 "his own worth and capabilities" (2.108).

己親屬 "his own kith and kin" (3.120).

己之本性 "his own inate nature" (7.83).

己力 "one's own strength" (2.84).

自己之民 "their own people" (2.95 (章)).

自己作孽者 "those who bring retribution on themselves" (2.88).

(d) For <u>Jii</u> preferred to the non-reflexive pronoun, see section 2.1.i above, Note. On the Mician slogan "I act in my own interests" the <u>Commentary</u> observes

為我為己也   (8.6).

4.6   AGENCY IN SUMMARY

LAC	LATE HAN	
	Changes in usage	Innovations in usage
吾;爾;etc. 或;莫	>我;汝 > Obsolete	或 becomes select-ive conjunction
偕 "both"	>俱 "all" 俱 encroaches on 皆 俱;皆 > collective before verbs	
孰 "which?" 相	>誰 "who?" 相 , but also occurs para-sitically	
交 為 自	> Obsolete, confused with 俱 謂 u.f. 為 Confined to reflexive roles	
己	Used with greater frequency	自己 etc.

The principal changes in the Agential Complex are shifts away from specialized forms, and their obsolescence, blunted usage, or parasitic retention, towards the use of single, all-purpose forms. These changes, as with those in syntagma and the verbal complex (see sections 2.7 and 3.7 above), are characteristics of the Archaic-Han Shift.

CHAPTER 5

CLAUSES, PHRASES AND ENDINGS
IN THE VERBAL SENTENCE

The principal changes in Late Han from LAC usage are:
(i) the diminution of the role of erl for subordination,
the re-introduction of the EAC form jih for subordination,
and a tendency to replace the erl clause of LAC, with a
greater complexity of clause assembly, and a greater variety of conjunctive devices (see 5.1); (ii) the parasitic occurrence of erl in the instrumental clause (see
5.2); (iii) greater complexity in clause assembly, leading to the redundance of the use of the anaphoric pronouns, with a consequent loss in both role and meaning
for the anaphoric pronouns, both singly and in combin-
ations (see 5.3); (iv) blunting in the use of the final
particles, and a tendency to reduce the variety of final
particles of LAC (see 5.4); (v) a new form of interrogative sentence (see 5.4.iii); (vi) changes in time and
place indications (see 5.5).

5.1. The Erl Clause
    i. Diminution in the role of Erl
    The erl clause, interposed between the agent and the
main verb, is of such common occurrence in LAC as to make
erl 而 one of its particles of highest frequency, and the
use of the erl clause a typical characteristic of LAC
(see LAC 3.7). In Late Han, by contrast, the role of erl
is almost exclusively conjunctive, usually adversative in
some sense, "yet, but" and the like, with the consequence
that erl clauses in the Text are very frequently rephrased
in the Commentary. In such cases, Jaw Chyi either dis-
regards erl altogether, or abstracts the subordinate

clause and restates it as a separate and coordinate
clause. <u>Erl</u> is then replaced by a wide variety of conjunctions, <u>yii</u> 以; <u>ru</u> 如; <u>tzer</u> 則; <u>shyh-yih</u> 是亦, etc.

Clearly, by Late Han times <u>erl</u> has lost much of the
precision of role and meaning it enjoys in LAC, and the
<u>erl</u> clause has been largely replaced by a greater com-
plexity of sentence structure. This greater complexity
affects not only the role of <u>erl</u> but also that of the
anaphoric pronouns, for which, see section 5.3 below.

<u>Examples</u>
(a) <u>Erl</u> disregarded
<u>Text</u> 王往而征之 "If having once set out, the King
were to punish them ..." becomes 願王往征之也
"wished the King to set out and punish them" (1.38);
<u>Text</u> 刺人而殺之 "Having stabbed a man, to kill
him" becomes 用兵殺人 "to kill a man with a weapon"
(1.31); <u>Text</u> 效死而民弗去 "If being faced with
death, the people do not leave [the city]" becomes
至死使民不畔去 "If, when death approaches, this
would not cause the people to leave [the city] in
rebellion" (2.22). Other examples will be found in
5.7, 1.94, 2.128 etc.
(b) <u>Erl</u> avoided, by breaking into two clauses
<u>Text</u> 用之而成路 "being put to use, it becomes a
road" becomes 用之不止則蹊成為路 "if used continually, then the footpath is made into a road"
(8.70); <u>Text</u> 四體不言而喻 "exemplified in every
limb, without being expressed in words" becomes 口
不言，人以曉喻而知之 "Nothing is said with the
mouth. But others, by the example manifested, know
about it" (7.99) (for the use of <u>erl</u> here in the
instrumental clause see section 5.2.i below); other
examples will be found in 2.84, 1.37, 1.40, 3.25,
2.17 etc.

ii. The use of the <u>Jih</u> Clause

On the other hand, where Jaw Chyi resorts to a sub-ordinate clause between agent and verb, he sometimes re-verts to the EAC form, using <u>jih</u> 既 (for this see <u>EAC</u> 3.7).

<u>Examples</u>

<u>Jih</u> marks a subordinate clause

孟子既為齊宣王言之滕文公問 "Mencius, having explained this matter for Duke Hsüan of Ch'i, was asked by Duke Wen of T'eng ..." (3.57); 人既自 有家復益韓魏百乘之家 "Men who, having estates of their own, further increase them with the hundred-chariot estates of Han and Wei ..." (7.85); 既不能得狂者欲得有介之人 "Being unable to get headstrong men, he wanted to get men of integrity ..." (8.114); 既不論三皇五帝殊無所問 "Not having discussed the Three Emperors and the Five Kings, there was absolutely nothing to inquire about" (1.48); 既去近留 , "Having left, to stay so close" (3.31). See also 6.107, etc. For other Late Han usages of <u>erl</u> see section 3.2.v above and 7.1.ii below.

<u>Note</u>. The subordinate clause in <u>jih</u> is a further ex-ample of the resuscitation of EAC forms in Late Han. See section 3.4.v Note, above.

5.2. The Instrumental

i. <u>Erl</u> terminating the Instrumental Clause

In LAC, the <u>erl</u> clause (... 而) is verbal, and the instrumental phrase (以 ...) is substantival. (See <u>LAC</u> 3.6.1; 3.7.1.) In Late Han the instrumental clause occurs sporadically with a parasitic <u>erl</u> (以 ... 而).

Examples

人以曉喻而知之 "Others, by the example manifested, know about it" (7.99); 故以相配而言之
也 "Therefore, by virtue of their respective suit-
ability, they are mentioned" (8.122); 不以性欲
而苟求之也 "does not, by following his natural
inclinations, seek improperly for them" (8.78); 以
己力不足而往服從於人 "to go and submit to
others because one's own strength is insufficient
[i.e., to resist]" (2.84). 以子噲不以天子之
命而擅以國與子之 "thinking that, Tzu-k'uai
had irresponsibly handed over the state to Tzu-chih,
not having done so with a charge from the Son of
Heaven" (3.8).

Note. For 謂 replacing 以 為 see section 4.4.i above.

5.3. Anaphora

i. The use of Anaphora

In the evolution from LAC to Late Han, the anaphoric
pronouns (pronouns used for repetition and recapitulat-
ion), chyi 其 and jy 之, become blunted and shift in meaning
(for which, see sections 2.1.i, 2.3.i-iv above). This
also happens to the allegro forms in which jy is incorporated (see paragraph ii below). But a more far-reach-
ing change takes place, of which the blunting and shift
of pronouns is but a symptom. This change is best
illustrated with an example. In 3.48 the following
passage occurs, which is here set out in a way so as to
show the order of its phrase and clause assembly, by
marking them from a to g; and to indicate the use of
anaphora in making connections of phrases, by underlining
the anaphoric pronouns.

諸侯之禮　**a**　The Rites for a Feudal Lord.

吾未之學也　**b**　I have not studied <u>them</u>.

雖然　**c**　Though <u>this</u> is so.

吾嘗聞之矣　**d**　I have learned <u>this</u> (i.e. the following.)

三年之喪　　⎧Three years of mourning,

齊疏之服　**e**⎨the wearing of mourning clothes,

飦粥之食　　⎩the eating of plain food,

自天子達於　**f**　from the Son of Heaven down to

庶人　　　　commoners,

三代共之　**g**　in the Three Dynasties, all practised <u>these</u>.

This passage is rendered in Late Han as follows, the rearrangement of clause and phrase being indicated by the use of the letters <u>a</u> to <u>g</u> (as above) within parenthesis.

我雖不學諸
侯之禮,嘗聞
師言三代以
前君臣皆行
三年之喪齋
疏齋食也

Though I have not studied the Rites for a Feudal Lord (<u>c</u> <u>b</u> <u>a</u>), I have heard my Master say (<u>d</u>) that, during and prior to the Three Dynasties, both Prince and Subject (<u>g</u> <u>f</u>) observed the three years' mourning period, mourning dress, and fasting (<u>e</u>).

Here, the rearrangement precludes the necessity for the use of recapitulatory pronouns.

In LAC, the anaphoric pronouns occur frequently and are used with precision and predictability. Their use is necessitated by the order of clause and phrase assembly. In Late Han a more supple order of assembly of phrase and clause reduces the necessity for the pronouns, and re-sults in an eroding of the distinctions made by the pro-nouns which, in LAC, are strictly observed.

<u>Note</u>. It might be thought that the difference between <u>Mencius</u> and its paraphrase, illustrated above, is merely

one of style. Mencius achieves an <u>effect</u> by the use of
disjointed phrases - a sort of range of emphases - while
Jaw Chyi achieves an <u>effect</u> of smooth transition by his
re-shuffling of the clause assembly. But if this is
merely stylistic change, it is of the nature of permanent
change, for it influences changes in the particles themselves. And it is not only the anaphoric pronouns that
suffer blunting and loss of role. The entire repertory
of grammatical particles display similar symptoms. Taken
together, this suggests a fundamental change in the
nature of the language which cannot be attributed merely
to stylistic variation. In their totality, these features add up to the Archaic-Han shift - a shift of the
grammatical burden borne by the "empty words" in LAC, to
the "full words" in Late Han.[1]

   ii. The eroding of the Anaphoric Pronouns
      in allegro forms

In LAC, the frequency of occurrence of the anaphoric
pronouns results, where there is constant collocation
with the post-verbal particle, in allegro forms. These
are <u>yan</u> 焉 (於 + 之) and <u>ju</u> 諸 (之 + 於 or 之 + 乎). <u>Yan</u>
and <u>ju</u> in the <u>Text</u> when rendered in the <u>Commentary</u> are
constantly misunderstood, leading to minor misinterpretations of the <u>Text</u>. When used freely (particularly in
the <u>Chapter Summaries</u>) <u>yan</u> and <u>ju</u> are either assimilated

---

[1] It might be added that when Jaw Chyi is writing
in Classical style as in the <u>Chapter Summaries</u> he
achieves the same effect of terse, disjointed phrases,
but either fails to use the anaphoric pronouns or mis-
uses them. This again suggests that the feature here
described is not purely one of style. (See Appendix 2.)

with the final particles, or used simply for 於之, or
used parasitically, in a way that suggests that by Late
Han they were no longer understood as allegro forms.

Examples

(a) 焉 in Text understood as "final particle" like 耳;
哉 etc.
Jaw Chyi defines 焉耳 in 1.20 as 焉耳者懇至之辭
"Yan eel are 'words' indicating emphatic finality."
The passage reads 盡心焉耳 "I exert my mind in it
[i.e. in governing my state] nothing more, nothing
less." Here yan is 於之 "in it," but Jaw Chyi reads
yan as being of a class with the final particle eel
耳. This understanding of yan colours the interpretation of many passages. 既竭心思焉 "having ex-
hausted the thoughts of the mind in it" becomes 盡
心欲行恩 "exhausting the mind, wishing to behave
with kindness" (4.74); 不藏怒焉 "does not harbour
resentment against him" becomes 不問善惡親愛之而已
"regardless of his behaving well or ill, loves him --
nothing less" (5.93); 何加焉 "what does that add to
me," becomes 何加益哉 "what increase is there?"
(6.113); 我不憾焉 "I am not vexed with him"(lit.
"by him") becomes 無恨心耳 "had no hatred in his
heart" (8.115).
(b) 焉 in Commentary used like 也 etc. or used parasitically. 其道一焉 "The Way is one!" (4.83 (章));
恥之甚焉 "This is the extreme of disgrace" (5.70
(章)); Text 則必取盈焉 "then must collect full
payment from them" becomes ... 必滿其常數焉 "They
must pay in full the average [assessment]" (3.62);
Text 何畏焉 "why be afraid of them" becomes 何畏齊
楚焉 "why be afraid of Ch'i and Ch'u?" (4.31.) In
the last two examples the yan in the Text is meaning-

ful, but as used in the <u>Commentary</u> it is tautologous
- - and thus parasitical.

(c) Misinterpretations arising from giving a wrong
interpretation to <u>yan</u> in the <u>Text</u>.   <u>Text</u>: 將為君
子焉 "there will be gentlemen in that place."   The
<u>Commentary</u> first observes 為有也 "<u>wei</u> is <u>yeou</u>" and
continues 有君子 "It has gentlemen" (3.73);   <u>Text</u>:
眊焉 "made dull by it," is understood as 眊然 and
defined as an attribute, 眊者蒙蒙目不明之貌
"the word <u>mau</u> means 'as though blindfold, the eye not
seeing'"(4.108);   <u>Text</u>: 納其貢稅焉   "took away
his revenues from him" becomes 納其貢賦與之
"collected his revenues, and presented them to him"
(5.93);   <u>Text</u>: 日月有明容光必照焉   "If the sun
or the moon is shining, their form and light are
always reflected in them" becomes 大明照幽微 "the
great lights [i.e. the sun and moon] shed light on
the dark and obscure" (8.5).

(d) 焉 is read as, or used as 於. 君子知舜告焉不
得而娶 "The True Gentleman knows that if Shun had
informed them, he would not have been able to marry"
(4.124.)   <u>Text</u>: 君無尤焉 "The prince should not im-
pute error to them" becomes 君無過責之 "The prince
should not scold them for their faults" (2.20).
Other examples of 焉 disregarded or misunderstood will
be found in 5.40, 5.61, 6.118, 6.104, 7.83, 7.76, 7.98,
8.51, 8.54, 1.40, 1.31, 2.124, 3.24, 3.85, 3.108,
2.107.

(e) The use of <u>ju</u>
<u>Ju</u> 諸 is replaced by <u>jy</u> 之 in 3.92, 1.79, 3.11.
<u>Ju</u> 諸 is used for <u>jy</u> 之 in 5.39.
<u>Ju</u> 諸 is replaced by <u>yu</u> 於 in 1.58.
<u>Ju</u> 諸 is replaced by <u>foou</u> 否 ; <u>jy-ye</u> 之邪 ; <u>jy-foou</u> 之
否 ; <u>jy-foou hu</u> 之否乎 ; <u>bu</u> 不; or <u>jy-hu</u> 之乎 in
5.105, 4.32, 5.116, 5.110, 1.72, 1.104, 2.7, 3.16.

5.4. The Final Particles

i. The loss of precision

The particles that occur at the end of sentences, and indicate the mood of the speaker, or impose an accentual pattern in LAC, are rendered with an abandon in the process of translation into Late Han that can only be described as chaotic. In LAC such particles are used with precision and predictability. In Late Han they lose this precision. If a statistical trend is of significance, Late Han seems to prefer ye 邪 for marking the interrogative; eel 耳 for marking heightened emotion (much more broadly than the 耳 = 而已 of LAC); and uses a new form of interrogative, final 不 and 否, for the alternative-choice sort of question.

Where final particles occur in allegro forms in LAC, (爾 for 而已；諸 for 之乎；與 for 也乎；夫 for 否乎 etc.) they are either misunderstood in Late Han or used interchangeably with single particles. Jaw Chyi, for example, defines 爾 as 爾者歎而不怨之辭 也 "The word eel is an interjection, but has no suggestion of resentment" (8.123), and 夫 as 歎辭 "a sigh-word," i.e. an interjection (6.64).

Thus the final particles, in common with many particles already described, display the same trend towards the erosion of meaning, the blunting of distinctions, and the reduction in role, that characterizes the Archaic-Han Shift.

Examples

Loss of precision in the use of the final particles. Hu 乎 is replaced by 也 as in 7.45, 6.46, 8.24; or by 否 as in 4.13, 5.128, 3.21; or by 邪 as in 3.87, 6.27, 7.24, 7.45, 3.37; or by 不 邪 as in 4.111; or by 也 乎 as in 8.123; and is supplied gratuitously in 3.24.

Hu is used for 哉 in 4.61; and for 與 in 6.28, 6.69.

Yü 與 by contrast is replaced by 矣 in 5.88; by 邪 in 6.68, 7.22, 6.81, 6.75; 6.64, 8.22, 8.91, 3.91, 4.59, 1.73, 6.68; by 也 in 4.59, 8.24, 6.68, 2.130; and used wrongly in 8.91; disregarded in 3.16, 2.5; replaced by 乎 in 2.123, 3.12; and replaced by 否 in 3.12.

Tzai 哉 is replaced by 乎 in 4.61, 3.12, 3.37; or by 也 in 6.26; or by 邪 in 6.103. Yee 也 and yih 矣 interchange in 3.82, 2.73, 5.8, 8.112 (twice) 8.2, 8.70, 1.28, 3.35.

Yee in Text is disregarded in 6.34.

Yih in Text is disregarded in 3.43.

Yee is supplied gratuitously in 6.76, 3.91, 6.41, 3.20, 3.21.

Yih is supplied gratuitously in 3.12.

Yee is replaced by eel 耳 6.111, 6.120, 5.38, 3.37.

Yee replaces 爾 in 5.25.

Yee is replaced by 邪 in 1.34; by 乎 in 3.22.

Erl-yii-yih 而已矣 in Text is replaced by 也 in 8.89, 8.83, and by eel 耳 in 8.21 and in 7.93.

ii. The use of Foou and Ran

In LAC ran 然 "it is so, yes!" and foou 否 "it is not so, no!" standing alone, are answers of consent or dissent to questions. Neither foou nor ran occur in this usage in Late Han. The paraphrist defines foou as 不是 in 5.117 (following Yuann Yuan's 阮元 emendation, see Jiau Shyun 正義 in loc.), and elsewhere almost invariably replaces foou with a material answer and paraphrases ran.

Examples

(a) Foou as a simple "no" in answer to a question is replaced by a material answer, or is explained 孟子言否云舜不詐喜 "When Mencius says 'foou' he

is saying that Shun did not feign his pleasure"
(5.88); <u>Text</u> 否 <u>Commentary</u> 言 不 然 也 "it means not so"
(5.97); <u>Text</u> 否 <u>Commentary</u> 堯 不 與 之 "Yao did not
give it "(5.105); <u>Text</u> 曰 否 <u>Commentary</u> 曰 不 自 織
布 "he said he did not weave the cloth himself"
(3.87); <u>Text</u> 否 <u>Commentary</u> 彭 更 曰 不 以 舜 為 泰 也
"P'eng Keng said 'I do not think Shun was gross'"
(4.20); and <u>Text</u> 曰 否 <u>Commentary</u> 彭 更 曰 不 然 也
"P'eng Keng said, 'It was not so'" (4.23).
(b) <u>Ran</u> as a simple "yes" in answer to a question is
replaced with a material answer. 以 鐵 耕 乎 曰 然
"Does he plough with a ploughshare?" He answered
'yes'." The answer here in the paraphrase is 相 曰
用 之 "Hsiang said 'He uses one'." (3.90); 然 "yes"
becomes 如 是 "as you say" in 3.53, 3.22, 3.16; see
also 7.6.

iii. <u>Foou</u> and <u>Bu</u> as final interrogatives

<u>Foou</u> 否 and <u>Bu</u> 不 (<u>bu</u> as an innovation) in Late Han,
however, occur at the end of sentences rendering them
interrogative, in an alternative-choice form of question-
ing.

<u>Examples</u>
(a) <u>Foou</u> 不 知 可 使 寡 人 得 相 見 否 "I do not know
if you can arrange for us to see each other or not?"
(2.117); 問 君 子 之 道 當 仕 否 "He asked, 'According to the way of the True Gentleman, is it obligat-
ory to give office [to a gentleman], or not?'"
(4.13); 知 肯 就 之 否 "[so that I may] know is he
willing to come or not?" (3.22); 不 知 誠 有 之 否
"I do not know if this is in fact so or not?" (1.51).
See also 3.90 and 3.21.
(b) <u>Bu</u> 足 以 笑 百 步 止 者 不 "Are they in an adequate position to mock those who stopped after

running a hundred paces?" (I.22); 王有是語不 "Did
your Majesty say this or not?" (1.72). See also
2.76, 6.113.

<u>Note</u>. The final interrogative <u>bu</u> in the above examples
is in certain editions replaced by <u>foou</u> 否. But final 不
can be attested as Han usage in other authors, for example in <u>Hann Shu</u>. See, for example, 楊樹達 詞詮 s.v. 不
p. 18 paragraph 5.

5.5. <u>Time and Place</u>

i. <u>Shyi</u> becomes obsolescent

The common indication of past time in LAC is <u>shyi</u> 昔
or <u>shyi-jee</u> 昔者 , which may indicate "yesterday," "a
few days ago," or "in far antiquity" (see <u>LAC</u> 3.10).
Wherever <u>shyi</u> is paraphrased it is replaced consistently.
For "yesterday" it is replaced by <u>tzwo-ryh</u> 昨日 (a Late
Han innovation), for "a few days ago" by <u>woang</u> 往 (昔
者往也, 謂數日之間也 <u>shyi</u> is <u>woang</u> and means "after
an interval of several days") (4.121) and for the far
past by <u>woang-jee</u> 往者. This is so consistent, that
<u>shyi</u> evidently was obsolescent in Late Han.

Examples
<u>Shyi-jee</u> or <u>shyi</u> is replaced by <u>tzwo-ryh</u> in 2.118
and 2.119, by <u>woang-ryh</u> in 2.4, and by <u>woang-jee</u> in
1.107, 1.94, 2.74, 3.29 and 5.64. See also 3.22.

<u>Note</u>.Wang Yih in his <u>Commentary</u> on the <u>Li Sau</u> also
explains <u>shyi</u> as <u>woang</u>. See Jiau Shyun's <u>Jenq-yih</u> 1.94.

ii. Miscellaneous

<u>Ta-ryh</u> 他日 "a day other than the day in question" is
defined as <u>yih-ryh</u> 異日 in 4.61 and <u>yih-ryh</u> replaces <u>ta-
ryh</u> in 4.62.

<u>Shyy</u> 始 is used equally in LAC and Late Han in the
time position for "prior to this" and in the aspectual

position for "for the first time." 始作俑者 is, however, rendered 李由有作俑者 (1.33) yielding been-you
"for first time" as an innovation in Late Han.

    Wei-jian 為間 for "after a short time, after an in-
terval" in both its occurrences in Mencius elicits comment from Jaw Chyi. In 3.124 he defines it as 有頃之
間也 and in 8.70 為間有間也; Jiau Shyun in his Jenq-
yih (3.125) observes that Gau Yow defines 有間 in Leu-
shyh Chuen-Chiou as 頃, and 間 in Jann-gwo Tseh as
須臾 and 有間 in Lieh Tzyy is defined as 小時也, which
suggests that 頃 and 須臾 had replaced wey jian by Late
Han times.

    Yu tzwu 於卒 and tzwu 卒 occur in LAC as "finally, in
the end." In 8.76 Jaw Chyi defines this as 卒後也 and
in 6.43 as 於卒末後復來時也. Jaw Chyi, however,
uses tzwu himself in 6.25 卒與之天位 "Finally, he
presented him with the Throne of Heaven." In 5.42 竟如
孫子之所言 "In the end, it transpired just as Ju Tzu
had said," jinq 竟 performs this function.

5.6   CLAUSES, PHRASES AND ENDINGS
        IN THE VERBAL SENTENCE IN SUMMARY

LAC	LATE HAN	
	Changes in usage	Innovations in usage
Erl clause	⎧ avoided ⎨ 既 for subord- ⎩ ination	
(以 ...)	(以 ... 而)	
焉　諸	⎫ Assimilated into ⎬ final particles, ⎪ use blunted, or ⎭ becomes parasitic	不　否 as final inter- rogatives
與　夫		
也　矣	⎫ Distinction ⎬ blunted ⎭	
昔	> 往	本　由 "for first time" 昨　日 "yesterday"

The verbal sentence of LAC, with its simple structure, its erl and instrumental clauses neatly demarked,
and its prolific use of resuming pronouns to indicate
the interrelationships of sentences, is thus replaced
with a looser, more complex clause and sentence structure. In this process, the anaphoric pronouns and erl
suffer diminution in role, semantic change, and blunting
of usage. This reduction in role is characteristic of
the Archaic-Han shift as has already been noted (see

sections 2.7, 3.9, 4.6, above). But it is also a characteristic of the Archaic-Han shift that sentences are
greatly expanded and their interrelationships are more
complex. These relationships are marked, not by resuming
pronouns and demonstratives, but by conjunctions. The
greater expansiveness of the sentence lessens the role
that the final particles of LAC play.

CHAPTER 6

T H E   D E T E R M I N A T I V E
S E N T E N C E

In the Determinative Sentence the principal changes
in Late Han from LAC usage are: (i) the establishment of
shyh as a copula in free or non-contrastive usage, the
introduction of dann as a copula, and the compounding of
the copulae of common inclusion; (ii) the introduction
of yuan as a causal particle.

6.1. The Copulae

i. Shyh as a Copula

Shyh 是 occurs as a copula in LAC, only as a contrastive form for fei 非 (see LAC 4.4.1). In Late Han shyh
occurs freely as a copula in the determinative sentence.

Examples

柳下是其號 也 "Liu-hsia is his courtesy name"
(2.108); 豈 非 皆 是 人 之 子 乎   "[Both
commoners and princes alike], surely it cannot but
be, all are somebody's son!" (8.24); 今此 時 亦 是
其 一 時 也 "Today, the present period is, too, one of
these periods" (3.35); 人 所 謂 是 舊 國 也 "What men
say is an ancient state ... " (2.3).

Note. Shyh also occurs freely in Late Han both as a
determinative demonstrative 是 仁 道 "this Humane Way"
(2.103), 是 詩 "this poem" (1.55); and as a pregnant
demonstrative 無 大 於 是 者 也 "There is nothing greater
than this" (2.121).

ii. Dann as a copula

In Late Han, dann 但 occurs between the two terms of
a determinative sentence in the sense of A is merely B,
and also (like fei 非 and shyh 是 in LAC) as the Determined
Term, in the sense of "It is merely ....." In this sense
both dann 但 and dann   wei 但為 occur.   The negated form
of dann in this usage is fei dann 非但.

Examples

(a) Dann as copula. 此亦但志食也 "This, after
all, is merely a matter of being concerned about
food" (4.22); 羽旄之美，但飾羽旄使之美好也
"The splendour of the feathered plumes is merely the
splendour of feather decorations" (1.77).

(b) Dann as Determined Term. 但義盡耳 "It is merely
a just thing pressed too far" (6.31); 但不以無為
有耳 "It is merely a matter of not taking the lack
for the possession" (2.82).

(c) Dann-wei as Determined Term. 但為合眾之行
"In fact, this is merely conforming with the crowd"
(8.115).   See also 1.99, 2.80.

(d) Dann negated with fei. 非但與姜女俱行而
已也 "It was not merely that he and the Lady Chiang
travelled together" (1.113). 人所謂是舊國也非
但見其有高大樹木也 "What men describe as
being an ancient state, is not merely one in which
tall trees can be seen" (2.3).   (When dann is negated
with bu it is determining a verb, as, for example, in
不但坐而聽命 "He does not merely sit, awaiting
the dictates of fate" (8.79).   Thus 不但 and 非但
contrast.)

iii. Jyi as a copula

Late Han uses jyi 即 as a copula, as does LAC, but jyi
before verbs in Late Han is aspectual (see 3.2.vi).

Examples

萬子即萬章也 "Wan Tzu is, in fact, Wan Chang"
(8.116); 離朱即離婁也 "Li Chu is, in fact, Li
Lou (4.64). 此即人之疢疾也 "This is, in fact,
the sickness of mankind" (7.95).

iv. Compounding of Copulae of Common Inclusion

The copulae of common inclusion (A is like B) of LAC
ru 如 ruoh 若 and you 猶 (but not you 由 which is obsolescent
in this usage in Late Han (see section 3.5.ii above)
occur unchanged in Late Han. When introducing a simile,
however, they tend to combine with pih 譬, thus pih-ru
譬如; pih-ruoh 譬若; and pih-you 譬猶

Examples
(a) Pih-ru. Text has ru but Commentary has pih-ru
in 8.84. See also 3.12, 8.108.
(b) Pih-ruoh. See 8.73, 7.93, 2.88, 3.116 (章).
(c) Pih-you. Text has you but Commentary has pih-you
in 4.87, 2.85.

6.2. Cause and Consequence
i. The use of Yuan

In 因 introduces a clause of cause in both LAC and
Late Han, in the sense of "because." Late Han also has
yuan 緣 with the same function and meaning.

Examples

後世緣此遂征商人 "In later generations, because of this, merchants were accordingly taxed"
(3.25); 聖人緣人心而制禮也 "The Sages, because
of human feelings, instituted [burial] rites" (3.123)
which is similar to 聖人緣情制禮奉終 "The
Sages because of human emotions, instituted rites for
the service of the dead" (3.125 (章)). See 2.82; 5.9.

<u>Note</u>. <u>Guh</u> 故 "cause" occurs before verbs in the sense
of "for good cause," "deliberately," "with something in
mind." <u>Yuan</u> is also used in this sense. 孟子雖心
知王意而故問者欲令王自道,遂緣以陳之
"Though Mencius knew in his heart what was in the King's
thoughts, he deliberately asked this question, because
he wanted to make the King say so himself. Accordingly,
with this in mind, he posed the question" (1.61). See
also section 2.5.i above, for the use of <u>jee</u> 者 in marking causal clauses.

6.3   THE DETERMINATIVE SENTENCE
IN SUMMARY

LAC	LATE HAN	
	Changes in usage	Innovations in usage
是 (in contrast to 非)	是 in free usage	但 ; 非但 譬如 ; 譬若 : 譬猶 .
如 ; 若 ; 猶 >		
由 >	Obsolescent	緣 (causal)

As with the verbal sentence (see section 5.6 above),
the Archaic Han Shift is marked in the Determinative
Sentence with a greater use of the connectives, which,
as with the conjunctions of the verbal sentence, come
into greater play as the clause structure becomes more
complex.

CHAPTER 7

C O N J U N C T I O N S

The principal changes in Late Han from LAC usage
among the conjunctions are: (i) The encroachment of
fuh 復 upon the role of yow 又 (see 7.1.i) and the development of adversative conjunctions (see 7.1.ii and iii).
(ii) The marking of both the protasis and the apodosis
in Conditional Clauses (see 7.2.i), the obsolescence of
goou 苟 , shinn 信 (see 7.2.ii) and sy 斯 (see 7.2.iii),
and the introduction of jiow 就 (see 7.2.v). (iii) The
introduction of new forms of concession, tzyh 自 for conditioned concession (see 7.3.i), taang 儻 for required
concession (see 7.3.ii), and shanq 尚 in a new form of
concession (see 7.3.iii).

7.1. Co-ordinate sequence

The conjunctions yow 又 "too, also" and yih 亦 "also,
after all" of LAC (see LAC 5.1) continue in use into Late
Han. The role of yow 又 , however, is encroached upon by
fuh 復 which, in this usage, is an innovation in Late Han.
Chiee 且 "moreover" also occurs as a conjunction, but in
its aspectual role shifts from potential to momentary
aspect (see section 3.2.i above).

i. Fuh as a Co-ordinate Conjunction

Yow 又 "and too, also, as well" in the Text is replaced by fuh 復 in the Commentary in 2.17, and by you-fuh
又 復 in 8.84. It occurs singly, and in the compounds
tzer-fuh 則 復 "and, furthermore," bwu-fuh 不 復 "but did
not also," and yow-fuh 又 復 "but in addition."

Examples

出疆何為復載質"When travelling beyond the
state frontier, why did he also carry a gift?"
(4.18); 今復并燕一倍之地 "but now, in add-
ition, you have incorporated territory from Yen ..."
(Text has 今又) (2.17); 追而還之,入蘭則可,又
復從而宵之 "having chased [the stray pig] and
returned it, and put it into its sty, that will do.
But to go on and hobble it as well ... (8.84); 但加
載書,不復歃血 "they merely attached the document
[to the sacrifice], but did not perform the blood-
smearing ceremony as well" (7.37); 父兄百官且復
言也 "His elders and officials, furthermore, said"--
Text has 且曰 ("furthermore said") (3.51); 被不
復問孰可,使自往伐之"They did not also ask me
'who should [attack Yen],' but, of their own volition, immediately went off and attacked it" (3.12).
See also 8.42, 3.106; etc.

ii. The Adversative

In section 5.1.i above, erl 而 is described as having
lost much of its LAC role and meaning in Late Han, and
to have shifted to use as a conjunction. In section
3.2.v one of those conjunctive functions is illustrated.
This is to supply the adversative, for clauses following
a dann clause (for example, 但食之而不愛 "merely to
feed him, but not to love him" (8.27)). But erl is not
confined to the adversative and occurs for simple connection "and" and for mild concession "yet."

In section 3.2.v Note above, two examples are cited,
which suggest that dann 但 by Late Han times is moving
towards its later use as an adversative conjunction.

Examples

(a) <u>Erl</u> as an adversative. 孔子以舜年五十而
思慕其親不怠稱曰孝之至矣 "Because Shun was
fifty years old, but still thought with sorrow of his
parents' neglect of him, Confucius called him 'the
filial son <u>par excellence</u>'" (7.15); 其人自以所
行為是而無仁義之實 "This sort of person
thinks his own course of conduct right, but lacks the
reality of Humanity and Justice" (8.117); 其富貴
已美矣而其人欲然不以足 "His wealth and
honours would already be of great splendour, but
such a man is indifferent and does not think this
enough" (7.85).

(b) <u>Erl</u> for simple connection. 其事遠而難 "These
matters are remote, and difficult" (4.98); 則通而
易 "then it is close at hand and easy of access"
(4.98 (章)).

(c) <u>Erl</u> for mild concession. 其好戰殘民與鄰國
同而猶望民之多 "He loved warfare and oppressed
his people, in just the same way as his neighbouring
rulers did, yet he still hoped for his population to
increase" (1.23). 李孫知孟子意不欲而心欲
使孟子就之 "Chi-sun knew that Mencius at heart
did not want to, yet still in his own mind he wanted
to make Mencius go [and accept]" (3.23).

iii. The use of <u>Faan</u> "on the contrary"
Late Han uses <u>faan</u> 反 "turn over, come back,"[1] in a

---

[1]<u>Faan</u> 反 in <u>Mencius</u> is used in the sense of "turn
over," literally, in the sense of "turning over the
hand" (e.g. in 2.39), figuratively, in sense of "turning
over in the mind - - reflecting upon" (e.g. in 2.55)
and in <u>faan fuh</u> 反覆 "over and over" repeatedly (e.g.

conjunctive usage, "to the contrary," which implies a
very strong adversative. This usage does not occur in
LAC.

Examples

若欲急長苗而反使之枯死也 "It is like want-
ing to hasten the growth of plants, but, on the
contrary, to cause them to wither to death" (2.66);
非徒無益於苗而反害之 "It is not merely of
no benefit to the plants, on the contrary, it harms
them" (2.68) (Text here has the conjunction yow 又
"but also"); 我欲行禮故不歷位而言反以我
為簡易也 "I wished to observe the Rites, and so
did not break ranks to speak [to him], but [he], to

_____

in 6.59.) Faan is used in the sense of "turn round,"
hence "to come back to" "to revert to" (e.g. in 3.43
and 8.119) and causatively "make come back" - - "return
property to" (2.18). In an extended sense it is used
for "return to, repay, requite" (e.g. in 2.51). It is
used in the sense of "turn against" hence "to contra-
vene" (e.g. in 3.49) and in faan donq 反動 "a reaction"
(see for example 2.59). In Late Han faan also occurs,
but for the series "come back to" "return to" etc. Late
Han prefers hwan 還 (5.64, 2.18, 3.32, 3.43, 8.24, 8.84,
etc.).

In other senses, baw 報 "to requite" (e.g. in
2.51) and guei 歸 "to revert to" (e.g. in 8.119) substitute for faan. Faan as a conjunction is, however,
an innovation in Late Han.

This study is restricted to a comparison of the
grammatical features in Text and Commentary. The
Commentary, however, offers - - as the above example
shows - - an excellent source for a historical study of
the development of the lexicon from Late Archaic to Han.

the contrary, thinks I behaved with laxity!" (5.53);
今之為闕反以征稅 "Frontiers today, on the
contrary, are used to impose taxes" (8.57); see also
4.22, 3.92, 4.89, 8.95 etc.

7.2. Conditioned Sequence

(a) Marking the Protasis

i. Ru-shyy, ru, jea-shyy and shyy

In conditioned sequences in LAC it is the apodosis
that is marked by conditional conjunctions. (See LAC
5.3.) The protasis has the verb modally determined by
ru如 ruoh 若 etc. But already in LAC (for example in Moh
Tzyy) these modal determinants with shyy 使 form a true
conjunction ruoh-shyy 若 使, and then precede the agent
of the protasis.

In Late Han, the conditional conjunctions marking the
protasis regularly precede the agent. They occur in the
forms ru-shyy 如使, ru 如, jea-shyy 假使 and shyy 使.
Shyy 使 in this usage is an innovation in Late Han.

Examples

Ru-shyy, jea-shyy, ru and shyy: 如使夷子葬其父
母也厚是以所賤之道奉其親也如其薄也
"If Yi Tzu buried his parents with extravagant rites,
then he was rendering service to his own kin in a way
he himself despises, but if he did so with inexpens-
ive rites ..." (3.119); 如使在王左右者皆非
居州之疇王當誰與為善乎 "If, among the
King's courtiers, no one is a man of the order of
[Hsüeh] Chü-chou, with whom can the King associate
in doing good?" (4.33); 如使賢者棄愚不養其
所當養則賢亦近愚矣 "If those who are compet-
ent abandon the inept, not looking after those whom
they should look after, then the competent themselves

are not far removed from the inept" (5.15); 使我得
志不居此堂也 "Even if I had my way, I would
not live in such houses" (8.101); 假使如子濯孺
子之得尹公之他而教之何由有逢蒙之禍
"Suppose now [that P'eng Meng had been taught by Yi
Yin] just as Tzu-cho Ju-tzu had been taught by Yin-
kung Chih-t'a how could the calamity of a P'eng Meng
have happened?" (5.42). See also 3.115, 6.120, 2.4,
2.116, 2.48, 2.73, 2.62, 2.80, etc.

ii. Cherng replaces Goou

In LAC, goou 苟 , shinn 信 and cherng 誠 , introducing
the protasis of a conditional statement, occur in the
sense of "If indeed, if in fact" etc. (see LAC 5.3.2).
Both goou and shinn in this usage are obsolescent in Late
Han. Goou is defined in 1.11 and 5.26 苟誠也 and is
consistently replaced by cherng, in the Commentary. In
one instance the replacement is inappropriate, for the
Text uses goou 苟 "improperly" in 不欲為苟去 "he did
not want, for an improper reason, to leave" which is
rendered 誠欲急去 "he really did want to leave quickly"
(7.30). LAC used shinn before verbs in a modal sense, as
an emphatic indicative. This, too, is replaced in Late
Han by cherng.

Examples
(a) Cherng replaces goou in 1.67, 2.24, 2.99 (twice);
4.31, 5.26, 5.48, 6.105 (twice); 7.56 (twice); 8.59,
8.91.
(b) Cherng replaces shinn in 2.94 and replaces
modal shinn in 水誠無分於東西 "Water indeed
does not differentiate between east and west,
but ..." (6.66).

(b) Marking the Apodosis

iii. Tzer 則 replaces Sy 斯

The protasis is typically marked in LAC by tzer 則
but, in Mencius, also by sy 斯. Sy is obsolescent in
Late Han, and is replaced by tzer 則.

Examples

Tzer replaces sy in 2.21, 1.31, 4.35, 5.9.

Tzer-sy replaces sy in 8.91 and occurs in 1.32 (章)

Sy-tzer replaces sy in 8.112.

Ruoh-tzer replaces sy in 6.27.

iv. Tzer replaced by Tsyy or Dang

Tzer 則 itself is replaced occasionally in Late Han
by tsyy 此 or dang 當.

Examples

Tzer is replaced by tsyy in 2.9.

Tzer is replaced by dang in 2.1, 2.2 (twice) and
2.19.

v. Jiow in Conditioned Sequences

Jiow 就 occurs in Late Han as a verb "to approach to"
"to come to" etc. and in this usage jiow occurs as early
as the Book of Songs. But in the two examples given
below, jiow seems close to its role in Modern Chinese.

Examples

(a) Jiow-shyy 就使 and jiow 就 as ? ruoh-shyy 若使
and ? tzer 則 堯舜之世皆行仁義故好戰殃
民者不能自容也就使慎子能使魯一戰取齊
南陽之地且猶不可 "In their day Yao and Shun
practised Humanity and Justice and so such things as
love of warfare and oppression of the people they
would not tolerate. If Shen Tzu can make Lu do

battle to recover the territory of Nanyang from
Ch'i, then that would be even more intolerable"
(7.42); 今之所謂君子,非真君子也. 順過
非就為之辭 "The so-called princes of today are
not true Princes. When they pursue an erroneous
course, or exhibit an impropriety, <u>then</u> they make
excuses for it" (3.18).

(b) Occurrences of <u>jiow</u> in verbal senses. <u>Jiow</u>
occurs as verb in 来就為卿 "when you came, you
became a minister" (3.20); 知肯就之否 "so that I
may know if he is willing to come or not?" (3.22);
see also 4.3, 7.35, 4.8 (章).

7.3. <u>Concession</u>

The Concessive Conjunctions <u>swei</u>雖 and <u>swei-ran</u> 雖
然 continue in use without change in Late Han. But two
important innovations are introduced for special kinds
of concession.

i. The use of <u>Tzyh</u>

<u>Tzyh</u>自 occurs as an innovation in Late Han[2] for con-
ditioned concession, in the sense of "even if, even
though" (see also section 3.5.i above).

<u>Examples</u>
此吾人者自有獻子之家富貴而復有德不
肯與獻子友也 "These five men, even though they
honoured the House of Hsien-Tzu as being rich and
noble but virtuous too, were unwilling to put themselves on the level of friendship with Hsien-tzu"

---

[2] <u>Tzyh</u>自 used for conditioned concession also
occurs in other Han writers. Examples occurring in
<u>Shyy-jih</u> (史記) and <u>Hann-shu</u> (漢書); for example,
will be found in Yang Shuh-dar, <u>Tsyr Chyuan</u> p. 364
<u>s.v. tzyh</u>.

(6.21). 管仲自魯囚執於士官, 桓公舉以為
相國 "Kuan Chung, even though in Lu he was impri-
soned by the Leader of the Knights, was promoted by
Duke Huan to the position of Premier" (7.59).

ii. <u>Taang</u> as a concessive conjunction
The introduction of <u>taang</u> 儻 to indicate a required
condition is also an innovation in Late Han. <u>Taang</u>
introduces a clause in the sense of "assuming that, provided that, always supposing that" etc.

<u>Examples</u>
如一見之, 儻得行道, 可以輔致霸王乎 "If once
he [Mencius] met with them [the Feudal Lords], provided that he was enabled to put his Way into effect,
could he not as a result assist them to become Para-
mount Prince?" (4.1). 王欲見之, 先朝, 使人往謂
孟子云寡人如就見者（言就孟子之舘相
見也）有惡寒之病, 不可見風, 儻可來朝欲
力疾臨視朝, 因得見孟子也 "The King wished to
see him [Mencius], so before dawn he sent a messenger to go and say to Mencius 'I was going to see you'
(i.e. he was going to Mencius' residence). But the
King had a cold, and could not expose himself to the
wind. Provided that [Mencius] could come to Court,
he would force [himself, despite] his illness,
graciously to see him there, and as a result, he
would [still] be able to see Mencius" (2.117).

iii. The use of <u>Shang</u> in Concession
<u>You</u> 猶 and <u>shang</u> 尚 (and <u>you-shang</u> 猶尚) occur in LAC
in a form of concession, in the sense of "even so, never-
theless" etc. (see <u>LAC</u> 5.4.3). <u>You</u> in this sense is
obsolescent in Late Han, its function being assimilated

into <u>shanq</u>. Shanq, however, occurs in a form of concession, in which an extreme case of something more
generally implied is conceded, often set off against the
general implication. <u>Shanq</u>, in such cases, occurs <u>after</u>
the statement of the extreme case.

<u>Examples</u>

仁者尚不肯為況戰鬪教人以求廣土地乎
"Even for a Humane man he would be unwilling to do
this, and how much less for one who murders people
by engaging in wars seeking thereby to enlarge his
territory?" (7.45); 陶器者少, 尚不可以為國,
況無君子之道乎 "Even when potters are in short
supply one cannot govern a state, how much less can
one do so without the Way of the True Gentleman?"
(7.51); 如是歌哭者尚能變俗 "Even such people
as these, singers and mourners, can change customs!"
(7.27); 虞人不得其招尚不往, 如何君子而
不待其招 "Even a huntsman, without the appropriate
summons, would not go, so what would be said of a
Gentleman who did not await the appropriate summons?"
(4.2); 周公太公地尚不能滿百里 "Even the
lands of the Duke of Chou and of the T'ai-kung could
not exceed a hundred miles square" (7.45).

7.4   CONJUNCTIONS IN SUMMARY

LAC	LATE HAN	
	Changes in usage	Innovations in usage
又 而 (subordinate) >	}又 復 而 (conjunctive)	反 (strongly adversative)
如 若 }(modal) >	如 若 }(conjunctive) 如使；假使	
苟 信 誠 } > 斯 (conditional)	obsolescent }誠 replaced by 則 此 當 }conditional	就 (for con-dition)
	自 (concession)	儻 (concess-ion)
猶 (concession) } 尚 >	尚 尚 ("even a")	

The conjunctions thus increase in variety, tend towards compounding, and enjoy far greater frequency of
occurrence. This, as has already been noted in 5.6 and
6.3 above, is characteristic of the Archaic-Han Shift.

CHAPTER 8

S U B S T I T U T I O N

The principal changes in Late Han from LAC among the
substitutes are: (i) The blunting of the distinction
made in the pronouns and demonstratives between determinative and pregnant forms, and the consequent obsoles-
ence of certain LAC forms and the weakening and blunting
of others (see 8.1 and 8.2). (ii) The obsolescence of
the interrogatives yan 焉 and u and u-hu 惡, 惡呼 and their
replacement by an 安 (see 8.3.i); the obsolescence of shi
奚 and shwu 孰 and their replacement by her 何 and shwei
誰 (see 8.3.iii, iv); the occurrence of her in new compound forms (see 8.3.v). (iii) The introduction of two
new interrogatives, ning 寧 and tserng 曾 (see 8.3.ii,
viii). (iv) Changes in the syntactical deployment of the
interrogative substitutes (see 8.3.vi).

8.1. The Pronouns
i. The Personal Pronouns
Two shifts, as already noted (see sections 2.1.i,
4.1.i above), occur from LAC to Late Han, in the use of
the personal pronouns. These are
(i) The tendency for the determinative forms wu and eel
to become assimilated with the pregnant forms woo and
ruu, and for the pregnant forms to assume indifferently
the agential and post-verbal roles.
(ii) When the personal pronouns are possessive, to mark
this with the particle of determination jy 之. This
gives

First person   <u>Pronoun</u>   <u>Possessive Adjective</u>

               <u>woo</u> 我   <u>woo-jy</u> 我之

Second person   <u>ruu</u> 汝   *<u>ruu-jy</u> 汝之

with a possibility, as variants, of <u>wu</u>吾 and <u>wu-jy</u>吾之 and <u>eel</u>爾 and <u>eel-jy</u>爾之

<u>Note 1</u>. In the Archaic-Han shift, therefore, the pronouns move perceptibly towards the <u>woo/woo-de</u> and <u>nii/ nii-de</u> of Modern Standard Chinese.

<u>Note 2</u>. Among the status pronouns (for which Jaw Chyi gives accurate descriptions, see Appendix 4), LAC <u>Goa-ren</u> 寡人 , used by princes when speaking of themselves, is consistently replaced by <u>woo</u>我 (and, in one instance, by <u>Chyi</u>齊 (i.e. "the King of Ch'i"); see 1.20, 1.110, 1.112, etc.

ii. The Anaphoric Pronouns

No shift, to parallel that of the personal pronouns, occurs in the anaphoric pronouns <u>chyi</u>其 and <u>jy</u>之 except that the differentiation between them is occasionally blurred (see section 2.2.i above). <u>Chyi</u>其 assumes a new demonstrative role (see section 2.3.ii). The main shift, as already described in section 5.3.i, is in the greatly reduced role played by anaphora itself. Because of this, the pronoun <u>jy</u>之 when incorporated into allegro forms, tends to become absorbed into the final particles (see section 5.3.ii above). This weakening leads, occasionally, to replacing <u>jy</u> in the <u>Text</u> by <u>tsyy-wuh</u> 此物 "this thing" or <u>tsyy-ren</u> 此人 "this person," <u>tsyy-shyh</u> 此事 "this happening" or, when <u>jy</u> is replacing a pronoun, by <u>jii</u> 己 "self," or <u>woo</u>我 "me."

<u>Examples</u>

<u>Text</u> 尊者賜之曰其所取之者義乎不義乎

<u>Commentary</u> 孟子曰今尊者賜己己問其所取此物

"Mencius said that if an honourable man gives a gift
to us and we ask from whom he obtained it ..." [lit.
"this thing"] (6.27); Text 何以謂之狂也 Commentary
何以謂此人為狂也 "Why did he call them [lit.
"these people"] headstrong?" (8.114); Text 士則茲
不悅 Commentary 士於此事不悅也 "As far as I
[i.e. Yin Shih] am concerned, this is displeasing
(3.31); Text 無處而餽之是貨之也 Commentary
義無所處而餽之是以貨財取我   "To give
a gift to me when no just occasion merits one is to
procure me with a bribe" (2.128); Text 竊聞之
Commentary 竊聞師言 "I heard [this >] my teacher
say" (2.75); Text 於傳有之 Commentary 於傳文有
是言 "In the Records handed down, there is this"
[i.e. these words) (1.80).

8.2. The Demonstratives

Mention, too, has already been made (section 2.3.i)
of the blunting of the distinction made in LAC between
determinative and pregnant forms of the demonstrative.
Sy 斯 and jy 之, the determinative demonstratives of LAC,
become obsolete, and tsyy 此 and shyh 是 play the major
role. Chyi 其, on the other hand, acquires a demonstrative role (see section 2.3.ii above).

8.3. The Interrogative Substitutes

The system of interrogative substitution, which, in
LAC, has forms restricted to and specialized in almost
every element in the sentence, tends in Late Han towards
the redundancy of specialized forms, and towards simpli-
fication, the substitute role converging on certain all-
purpose interrogatives. Thus yan 焉 and u 惡 u-hu 惡呼 in
the Time and Place position are assimilated into an 安;
the distinction between shwu 孰 and shwei 誰 is blurred

and the role of both is assumed by <u>shwei</u>. Shi 奚 <u>her</u> 曷
and <u>hwu</u> 胡 become obsolescent, and are replaced by the
all-purpose <u>her</u> 何.

There is, too, parallel with similar developments
already described elsewhere, a tendency towards the use
of periphrasis (<u>her</u> 何, for example, is expanded according to need to <u>her-deeng</u> 何等, <u>her-ren</u> 何人, etc.) and
a tendency for substitutes to occur after the verb,
where, in LAC because of polarity, they occur before
the verb, as for example when <u>her-wey</u> 何謂 becomes <u>wey-
her</u> 謂何, <u>shwei</u> <u>yeu</u> 誰與 becomes <u>yeu</u> <u>shwei</u> 與誰, and
forms like <u>yun-her</u> 云何 occur.

Late Han also has two new interrogatives <u>ninq</u> 寧 and
<u>tserng</u> 曾.

i. The assimilation by <u>An</u> of <u>Yan</u> and <u>U</u>
   and <u>U-hu</u>

In LAC <u>yan</u> 焉 occurs in the Time and Place position,
and asks "when?" "what time for?" "where?" and "whither?"
<u>U</u> 惡 and <u>u-hu</u> 惡呼 in the Place position substitute for
the element that appears, in non-interrogative statements, in the second post-verbal position. They ask
"where?" "whither?" but also "by whom?" or "by what?"
where the verb is passive.

In Late Han both <u>yan</u> and <u>u</u> are obsolete, and are replaced by the all-purpose <u>an</u> 安.

<u>Examples</u>
(a) <u>Yan</u> is replaced by <u>an</u> in 8.52, 5.7, 4.103, 4.109,
2.128, 4.10.
(b) <u>U</u> and <u>u-hu</u> are replaced by <u>an</u> in 8.15, 4.126,
4.109, 6.38, 7.53, 1.88, 1.41, 3.22, 1.33, 3.63,
3.86, 3.117, 4.61, 3.32.
(c) <u>An</u> occurs in <u>Commentary</u> in 2.16, 6.51, 8.119,
8.98.

(d) <u>Her</u> substitutes for <u>yan</u> in 8.3, 2.103, 2.108.

(e) <u>Her</u> substitutes for <u>u</u> in 2.123.

(f) <u>Chii</u> substitutes for <u>u</u> in 8.22.

<u>Note</u>.U 惡 as an interjection is also obsolescent in Late Han. It is defined as a "deep sigh" in 2.121, "an interjection expressing unease" in 2.74, and is replaced by the verb <u>tann</u> 歎 "to sigh" in 3.14.

ii. The use of <u>Ninq</u>

An 安 occurs in the Time and Place position in Late Han as an interrogative substitute. <u>Ninq</u> 寧 (which shares certain affinities with <u>an</u>, for example both mean "peace, to pacify") occurs in Late Han as an interrogative substitute in the position occupied by such words as <u>kee</u> 可 <u>neng</u> 能, expressing ability, possibility, and the like. <u>Ninq</u> in such contexts asks "could?" "can?"

<u>Note</u>.Ninq occurs in the <u>Commentary</u> as a verb in 8.16 "bring peace to." In its other occurrences it is (i) interrogative and (ii) in the "agential state" position. It is tempting to regard <u>ninq</u> as an interrogative form of <u>neng</u> (*nieng, *nəng). None of the conventional dictionary definitions of <u>ninq</u> (as, for example, <u>Tsyr Hae</u> 願詞 "expressing wish or preference"; 何也 "how?"; <u>chii</u> 豈也 "surely not?") account adequately for Jaw Chyi's use of <u>ninq</u>.

<u>Examples</u>
<u>Text</u> 可得聞與 "could I hear about that?" becomes 寧可得聞邪 (1.73). <u>Text</u> 有諸 "was there such a thing?" becomes 寧有之 "could such a thing be?" (1.79). <u>Text</u> 雖欲耕得乎 "Even though he wanted to plough, could he have managed to?" becomes 寧得耕乎 "would he have been able to plough?" (3.97). <u>Text</u> 可復許乎 "could [you] promise to bring them

about once more?" becomes 寧可復興乎 "Could [you]
once again revive?" (Jaw Chyi explains 許猶興也
hence his interpretation of this sentence) (2.35).
Text 如此則動心否乎 "If this happened, would
you be moved or not?" becomes 如是寧動心畏難
"If this happened, could you be moved, or have fear
for difficulties?" (2.48). Other examples occur in
3.90, 1.106, 6.27, 7.4.

iii. The assimilation of Shwu by Shwei

The assimilation of the agential distributive interrogative shwu 孰 into the more general interrogative substitute shwei 誰 has already been described in section
4.2.iv above.

iv. The obsolescence of Shi 奚

Jaw Chyi defines shi 奚 in 5.87 as 奚何也 and consistently replaces shi in the Text by her. Where shi-
wey 奚為 occurs in the Text it is replaced by her-wey
何為 , but her-wey also occurs as a replacement for shi
alone. Shi evidently is obsolescent in Late Han.

Examples
Her replaces shi in 3.89, 8.19, 6.33, 7.8, 7.4, 1.69,
8.73.
Her-wey replaces shi-wey in 3.89, 7.55, 2.15, 2.31.
Her-wey replaces shi in 5.55, 6.34, 5.87.

v. Expansions of LAC Her

Her 何 substitutes at all levels, syntagmatic, sentential, and intra-sentential in LAC (see LAC 6.5). In
Late Han certain of these levels are differentiated by
periphrasis.

Where, in LAC, her occurs before a noun, in sense of
"what sort of" "what kind of," Late Han has her-deeng 何

等 ; where <u>her</u> occurs in LAC in sense of "what can be said about," Late Han has <u>yun-her</u> 云何 . Both <u>deeng</u> and <u>yun</u> in these senses are innovations in Late Han.

Examples

<u>Text</u> 何人也 "what kind of person is he?" becomes 何等人也 (8.81); 不善之實何等也   "of what sort is the reality behind the word" '<u>bu-shan</u>'?" (5.24).   <u>Text</u> <u>ru her</u> 如何 "what can be said about it" becomes 其事云何· "of this happening, what can be said?" i.e. "what do you think about this matter?" (5.107). 鄉原之惡云何   "What can be said about the evil of the 'honest villagers'" (8.115) (<u>Text</u> has 何如). See also 2.50, 2.59, 2.61.

<u>Note 1.</u> Yun occurs in LAC to indicate quotation. In Late Han it occurs as a verb "to speak" as does <u>wey</u> 謂 in LAC, as, for example, 亦云太甚   "that, too, would be called excessive" (8.84); 孟子云 "Mencius said ..." (6.52, 7.27, etc.); hence <u>yun-ho</u>, 云何 "say what?" i.e. "what can be said about?"

<u>Note 2.</u> Her-you 何由 in LAC asks "from whence?" (see <u>LAC</u> 6.5.2.2). <u>You</u> 由 for "from" is obsolescent in Late Han (see section 3.5.ii above). Late Han uses <u>you</u> 由 in the sense of <u>yong</u> 用 and hence <u>her-you</u> 何由 in the sense of "of what use?" Examples are 教人治國不以其道則何由能治者乎 "If one were to instruct a man to govern the State contrary to the way [he has been taught], then of what use is his ability to govern?" (2.10); 侮奪之惡何由干之而錯其心· "The evils of arrogance and of acquisitiveness - - of what use is it to confound the mind by being involved in these things?" (4.110 (章)); 當以時修橋梁民何由病苦涉水乎 "He [i.e. Tzu-ch'an] should have repaired the bridges at the proper time and then what use would the people have

for crossing rivers with such pain and suffering?" (5.6).

    vi. Changes in the syntactical deployment
       of the Interrogative Substitutes

In LAC, pronominal substitutes occurring after the
verb shift to the pre-verbal position when polarity is
involved. In interrogative statements, the interrogative, in comparable deployment, also shifts to the pre-
verbal position. In Late Han, this shift does not always
occur.

    <u>Examples</u>
    <u>Text</u> 何謂 becomes 謂何 in 8.81, 2.70 (see also 2.79,
2.19, etc). See also preceding paragraph where <u>her</u>
occurs after <u>yun</u>, viz. 云何 . . <u>Text</u> 何以 becomes
以何 (6.52). <u>Text</u> 誰敬 "to whom should I show
respect?" becomes 敬誰 (6.76). 誰先 "to whom should
I give precedence?" becomes 先酌誰 "to whom
should I give precedence when offering wine?" (6.77).

    <u>Note.</u> This shift is consonant with the shifts occurr-
ing through the obsolescence of the <u>negative/substitute/</u>
<u>verb</u> type of polarity (see section 3.6.i above).

    vii. The use of <u>Chii</u>
    <u>Chii</u> 豈 occurs in LAC where a question is rhetorical
and anticipates a negative answer. <u>Chii</u> occurs in this
usage also in Late Han, but the paraphrase often gratuitously adds <u>chii</u> where it is not in the <u>Text</u>. <u>Chii</u>,
thus, is evidently current usage in Late Han.

    <u>Examples</u>
<u>Chii</u> occurs in the <u>Commentary</u> but not in the <u>Text</u>
in 7.57, 7.51, 6.52, 8.24, 8.73, 7.92, 8.30, etc.
In 豈可得聞與 "May I hear about that?" (2.56),
<u>chii</u> seems to be purely interrogative without the
implication of an answer in the negative.

viii. The use of Tserng

Tserng 曾 occurs before bu 不 twice in the Commentary. Tserng is described in the Fang Yan (方言) as her-wey 何為 (see Tsyr-hae s.v. tserng). This appears to be the best interpretation to be placed on the following two examples: 剌邠君曾不如此鳥 "[The Duke of Chou, in writing this Song] wanted to needle [= criticize] the Prince of Pin [by asking] why did [he] not emulate this bird?" (2.87); 而曾不閔 "so why should he not mourn?" (7.15).

Note. The Tsyr-hae entry, quoted above, cites the Shin Fang-yan Shyh-tsyr 新方言釋詞 as authority for the suggestion that tzeen 怎 is a vulgar variant of tserng. Under tzeen, the Tsyr-hae notes that in T'ang poetry jeng 爭 is used for tzeen.

8.4.   SUBSTITUTION IN SUMMARY

LAC	LATE HAN	
	Changes in usage	Innovations in usage
焉;惡 and 惡呼 孰/誰 > 奚 > 何	> 安 誰 > 何	寧 "could?"
		>何等; 何人 etc.
何由 "from whence?"	何由 "of what use?"	
何謂 etc. 豈	謂何 etc. 豈 (in broader usage)	曾 "why"

The interrogative substitutes, therefore, in common
with other substitutes, share in the common shift away
from specialized forms towards all-purpose forms, and in
the tendency for the all-purpose forms to combine in
compound forms.

CHAPTER 9

M I S C E L L A N E O U S

Other shifts and innovations in Late Han from LAC
concern the degrees of comparison, the allegro forms,
and enumeration. These are (i) new periphrastic means
for indicating the degrees of comparison, and a tendency
to mark comparison, where, in LAC, it is often unmarked;
(ii) an avoidance of the use of allegro forms; (iii) the
use of <u>deeng</u> 等 in the sense of "et cetera."

1. The Degrees of Comparison

The comparative and superlative degrees of comparison are as often as not unmarked in LAC, though LAC has
the resources for marking them. In Late Han the degrees
are more frequently marked, and new forms occur for marking them.

Preceding the attribute, LAC has <u>jia</u> 加 and <u>yih</u> 益.
Late Han has also <u>tzeng</u> 增.

Examples

<u>Text</u> 民不加少 "My population does not get any
larger" becomes 民人不增多於鄰國 "My population
does not get any larger than my neighbours" (1.21);
益甚 "even more serious" (2.14) (see also 2.39);
而加撫恤之 "and sympathize the more with him"
(1.78).

Following the attribute, with the particle of determination, LAC has <u>jy shenn</u> 之甚 ; <u>jy jyh</u> 之至 ; and <u>jy
you</u> 之尤 . Late Han avoids these formations and explains
the use of <u>jyh</u> 至 in them as <u>jyi</u> 極 (5.103 and 4.80). Late
Han prefers the inverted form.

Examples

至要 "most important" (2.58)

甚白 "very white" (3.112)

甚過 "very much in error" (7.52)

In the superlative degree, LAC has unmarked attributes. For example, meei = "lovely" in 牛山之木美矣
"The trees of Bull Mountain were once lovely" (6.102).
Meei = "lovelier" or "better" in 膾炙與羊棗孰美
"Which is the better [eating], cooked meat or dates?"
(8.105) and meei = "loveliest," "best" in 五穀者種
之美者也 "The five grains are the best among plants"
(6.129). Meei also occurs in an excessive degree "too
lovely, too elegant" as in 木若以美然 "The wood, it
seems, was too elegant" (3.1).

To mark the superlative degree Late Han has tzuey 最

Examples

Text 仁為美 "Humanity is its loveliest attribute"
becomes 仁最其美者也 (2.102); Text 莫近焉
"Nothing is closer than that" becomes 最為近 "[This
is] the closest" (7.75); 最為違禮 "running contrary to ritual, in an extreme degree" (8.83).

To mark the excessive degree, Late Han has Tay 泰太.

Examples

Text 木若以美然 "the wood, it seems, was too
elegant" becomes 木若以泰美然也 (3.1); 齊宣
王以三年之喪為太長久 "King Hsuan of Ch'i
thought that three years of mourning was too long"
(8.30). See also 太重 "too much" 太輕 "too little"
(8.98); 太隘狹 "too narrow-minded" (2.112); 太過
"excessive" (2.82).

2. The Allegro Forms

In general the allegro forms of LAC, which combine
in a portmanteau form two commonly associated particles,
are either used in Late Han in blunted senses or become
obsolete. The following is a list of allegro forms
which occur in <u>Text</u> and <u>Commentary</u>:

LAC	LATE HAN
<u>eel</u> 爾（而已 ）	prefers 耳 which is often used as a meaningless enclitic
<u>eel</u> 耳（而已 ）	see above
<u>fwu</u> 夫（否乎 ）	prefers <u>foou hu</u>
<u>her</u> 盍（何不 ）	acceptable
<u>her</u> 曷（ ? ? ）	avoids
<u>hwu</u> 胡（何故 ）	avoids
<u>yan</u> 焉（於之 ）	avoids
<u>in</u> 因（用以 ）	acceptable
<u>iu</u> 諸（之於 ）	avoids
<u>nae</u> 乃（若茲 ）	acceptable
<u>ran</u> 然（如此 ）	avoids in non-combining sense, e.g. as "just so"
<u>shi</u> 奚（何以 ）	avoids
<u>u</u> 惡（何於 ）	avoids
<u>yu</u> 與（也乎 ）	avoids
<u>ye</u> 邪（也乎 ）	very common, but often, simply interrogative

3. Enumeration

In lists of names, where the list is not completed,
Late Han uses <u>deeng</u> 等 "equal, on a par," as a sort of
"et cetera," <u>deeng</u> substituting for the names unstated,
but to be assumed by the reader. This is an innovation
in Late Han.

4.   MISCELLANEOUS IN SUMMARY

LAC	LATE HAN	
	Changes in usage	Innovations in usage
<u>Jia</u> 加x; 益 <u>yih</u> x		<u>tzeng</u> 增 x 太, 泰, 最. <u>deeng</u> 等 "etc."

CHAPTER 10

C O N C L U S I O N

Reviewing now the features described in chapters 2 - 9,
the nature and extent of evolutionary change in the
grammar of the language from the 3rd century B.C. to the
2nd century A.D. might be summarized as follows:

1. The "empty words" suffer loss in role and meaning.
More specifically: (i) There is a diminution in the role
played by "empty words" in making grammatical distinctions. (ii) There is a reduction in the number of distinctions made by the "empty words" and in the number
itself of "empty words" employed and a tendency for those
employed to be used in blunted or broadened senses. The
trend is towards general all-purpose forms. (iii) There
is semantic loss in certain "empty words" leading to
their employment in parasitic or meaninglessly enclitic
ways. (iv) There is also semantic shift in certain auxiliaries leading to shifts in role and deployment.
2. There is an increase in the use of periphrastic means
to make grammatical distinctions. More specifically,
the formal means of indicating the determinative role,
of indicating mood, voice, and interrogation and the
like, which are vested in the "empty words" of LAC, are
replaced in Late Han by periphrasis, and new periphrastic
forms occur.
3. The "full words" acquire enhanced significance. More
specifically, the single word of LAC tends to be replaced
by the compound word in Late Han and the compound word
tends to greater restriction in grammatical deployment.
Words customarily occur in either nounal or verbal
positions, and do not permutate.

A major evolutionary shift, therefore, occurs between the 3rd century B.C. and the 2nd century A.D.
The "Archaic-Han Shift" is away from the precise, predictable, and meaningful use of the "empty words" and
a reduction in their grammatical role, with a corres-
ponding increase in the more precise indications and
predictable deployment of the "full words". Quite
clearly during these critical five hundred years a
change of the greatest importance in the historical
evolution of the language takes place. We might say
that the traditional characterization of the grammatical
auxiliaries of Chinese as "empty words" in Archaic
Chinese is a misnomer, but that once the Archaic-Han
Shift takes place, the characterization become appropriate. The seeming "modernity" of certain Han innovations has been remarked upon. What is here called the
"Archaic-Han Shift" is towards features that are recog-
nizably typical of Modern Standard Chinese.

But there is also a retrogressive tendency observable in the history of "Classical Chinese" in Han times.
While writers like Jaw Chyi, and, later, the author of
the Shyh-shuo Shin-yeu (世說新語) and the like, reflect, in their "easy wen-yan," the evolutionary move-
ment in the language, others, like Ban Guh in Hann Shu
and Jaw Chyi himself in the Chapter Summaries, in deference to canonical authority, embellish their writings
with archaic forms and particles and follow an artificial
metrical pattern in deliberate imitation of classical
models. It is thanks therefore to the Commentary of Jaw
Chyi that we can measure the extent of obsolescence,
innovation, and change. If we had to depend upon the
great Han Classicists, with their admixtures of the old
and the new, the task would be much more difficult.

POSTSCRIPT

In paragraph iii of the Introduction to this book the statement is made that "a number of features have been described as 'Late Han innovations,' which must be understood in an accommodated sense. They are innovations in so far as Archaic Chinese is concerned, but they may well have antedated our Late Han author."

In the Leu-shyh Chuen-chiou, Mr. Ward informs me, a text which dates from the very close of the Late Archaic period, the following features occur, which elsewhere in this book have been described as Han innovations.

(i)   The introduction of the protasis in a conditional sequence, in the pre-agential position by 若 ; 使 ; 為 ; 若令 ; and 今使 . (cf. 7.2.i).

(ii)   The use of 有閒 (cf. 5.5.ii).

(iii)   The 被 and 為 passive (cf. 3.4.i).

(iv)   The occurrence of " 如 ... 如 ... " for "either... or..." (cf. 4.2.i).

(v)   The use of 反 "on the contrary". (cf. 7.1.iii).

(vi)   The use of 其卒 and 其餘 . (cf. 2.3.iii).

(vii)   The blunting of the 其 and 之 distinction. (cf. 2.2.i).

(viii) The use of 最 , and the occurrence of 甚 and 至 before attributes. (cf. 9.1).

With these exceptions, the Leu-shyh Chuen-chiou is, in every other linguistic respect, a typical Late Archaic document, as the transitions which its Late Han commentator Gau Yeou makes, testifies (see footnote 13).

APPENDIX 1

LATE HAN AND EARLY ARCHAIC CHINESE

The Shu Jing and the Shy Jing, which are Early Archaic texts, are frequently cited in Mencius, and, where such citations occur, Jaw Chyi in his Commentary translates them into Late Han.

His treatment of the grammatical auxiliaries of EAC is as follows:

Chapter and paragraph in Early Archaic Chinese	Early Archaic		Late Han	Reference in Mencius
	Shu Jing	Shy Jing		
Syntagma				
2.5		及	與	1.112
2.6.7.1	歐		其	1.90
2.6.7.3		靡	無	4.88
Verbal Sentence				
3.3.ii	丕		大	4.46
3.3.2.7	一		初	2.15
3.3.3.2		哿	可	1.109
3.4	于	于	於	6.28, 4.30 1.88
	越		於	6.28
3.4.5.1	自	自	從	2.85, 5.110
3.5.3	咸		皆俱	4.46 1.113
3.5.3.1		聿或	誰無	2.87 6.28
	亡	莫	無有	5.100

Chapter and paragraph in Early Archaic Chinese	Early Archaic		Late Han	Reference in Mencius
	Shu Jing	Shy Jing		
3.5.4	骨	骨	相	1.98, 1.113, 4.96
3.5.5	β/del/ə'		del/β	1.89
3.6	其		以	1.89
3.7		其	而	3.56
3.9		戡	[辭也]	4.96
3.10		普	徧	5.100
		迨	及	2.87
		于時	於是時	1.86
Determinative Sentence				
4.2	惟		作	1.89
Inter- Sentential				
5.4.1	乃		由是	1.98
5.4.2	其		則	2.15
Substitution				
6.2	厥		其	1.90
		言	我	2.88
6.4	時		是	1.18
6.5	害		大	1.18
		爰為	何為	2.14
			何	1.88, 1.89
6.6	曷攸		所	3.67, 4.28
Miscellaneous				
7		爰	於是	1.88, 1.113
			又以	1.110

In column four above, "Late Han," it will be seen
that the language that Jaw Chyi uses for paraphrasing
EAC is precisely the same language that he uses for
paraphrasing LAC. Consistency and predictability are
thus maintained throughout the Commentary.

A comparison of EAC and Late Han confirms the con-
clusions already drawn as to the nature of evolutionary
change in the language from LAC to Late Han. The obsolescence of specialized forms of the pronouns and demonstratives, and the convergence upon all-purpose forms,
are shown in the rendering of yan 言 jyue 厥 and shyr 時
by the all-purpose woo 我 chyi 其 and shyh 是 ; the distributives yuh 聿 and huoo 或 by the all-purpose, but
blunted, jiu 俱 and shwei 誰 ; the interrogative and in-
definite substitutes her 曷 shi-wey 奚 為 and iou 攸 by
the all-purpose her 何 and suoo 所 . The allegro forms
are rendered in their discrete parts, for example, yuan
爰 by yu-shyh 於 是 . The special negatives mii 靡 wang 亡
and moh 莫 are replaced by wu 無 .

Jaw Chyi betrays a considerable understanding of both
Early Archaic and of Late Archaic, but Archaic Chinese is
not without its difficulties for him. He misunderstands
the EAC hay 害 (allegro form of her-yii 何 以) rendering
it as dah 大 "great." But he cites, in his Commentary,
glosses on the Shy Jing of both the San Jia 三 家 and the
Mau 毛 schools (2.87, 1.113, etc.). He independently quotes
from the Shu Jing (5.2, 5.30, 4.42, 3.95, etc.) and is
familiar with the 古 尚 書 in 120 chapters (see 4.29 and
5.74). He cites the Tzuoo-juann (5.39, 2.131, 3.26,
etc.); Analects (6.58, 3.46, 6.107, etc.); the Shiaw
Jing (6.83); the Jou Lii (3.71, 3.73, 3.77, etc.), and
the Yih Jing (7.53, 8.29, 8.78), in addition to his
identifications of, and provision of references for,

citations from the <u>Shu Jing</u> and <u>Shy Jing</u> in the <u>Text</u>.[1]
We must suppose him to have been a well-read man.

------

[1] For the identification of the sources of Jaw
Chyi's glosses I am indebted to the magnificent text-
critical study of the text of <u>Mencius</u> and of the Jaw
Chyi <u>Commentary</u> by Jiau Shyan (see footnote 13 above).

APPENDIX 2

THE NATURE OF LATE HAN
CLASSICAL CHINESE

The language used by Jaw Chyi for paraphrase in his
Commentary is quite different from the language he uses
for the Chapter Summaries in which, at the close of each
chapter, he points up the moral he wishes to draw from
the Text. This difference in language I have characterized as Late Han Literary Chinese and Late Han Classical
Chinese respectively.

Late Han Literary Chinese confines itself to contemporary grammatical forms, is free and uncontrived but
prolix. Late Han Classical Chinese borrows from Archaic
grammatical forms, is mannered, patterned, and terse.

Late Han Classical Chinese is restricted to a line
of four stresses or of multiples of four - - eight or
twelve - - with an introductory or concluding line which
is metrically irregular. This metrical restriction im-
poses economy in the use of the "empty words." But when
the "empty words" occur, they are drawn from a repertory
composed, indifferently, of Early, Middle and Late
Archaic forms, but also including contemporary forms.
Late Han Classical Chinese therefore is not an attempt
to imitate Archaic Chinese with any consistency, but a
style in which Archaic features provide stylistic variants for contemporary features, thus providing a "classical" flavour.

In the Chapter Summaries, both Early and Late Archaic
forms, which Jaw Chyi is so careful to avoid in the
Commentary, are freely used. That they are used to
achieve a "classical effect" is shown by their occasional

occurrence in contexts where they are not, strictly
speaking, appropriate. For example, the LAC <u>tzyh</u> 自
"from" which is avoided in the <u>Commentary</u> as obsolescent,
and replaced by <u>tsorng</u> 從 "from," occurs in the <u>Chapter
Summaries</u> as a variant for <u>tsorng</u> 從 "to follow," "con-
form with" etc., a usage which is foreign to LAC, but
which derives from Jaw Chyi's definition of 自 as 從 (see
8.48 below). Examples of Archaic features used in Late
Han Classical style are as follows:

1. Early Archaic Features

匪 ; in 匪禮之踰 for 非 禮 "the excesses of improper Rites" (3.8 (章)) (see also 4.125).

攸 ; in 人倫攸敍 for 所敍 "the order in which
human relationships are placed" (8.125 (章)).

茲 ; in 諸侯如茲 for 如 此 "if the Feudal Lords
behaved thus" (8.88 (章)).

2. Late Archaic Features

孰 ; in 孰敢不正 for 誰 敢 "who dare not correct
himself" (8.120 (章)).

自 ; in 不自王命 for 從命 "not according to the
King's command" (8.48 (章)).

斯 ; in 亦斯類也 for 此 類 "[these] too, are of this
kind" (8.2 (章)).

諸 ; in 不反諸己 for 之於己 "not seek it in himself" (6.129 (章)).

弗 ; in 聖意弗珍 for 不珍 "the thoughts of the
Sages were not prized" (1.70 (章)).

勿 ; in 惡而勿去 for 不去 "to hate it, yet not to
leave" (4.83 (章)).

　　　See also 斯亦 used for 此 亦 ; (8.125 (章)).

自 used for 從 ; (4.83 (章)).

尚 used for 當 ; (8.38 (章)).

斯 used for 則 ; (7.77 (章)).

3. Contemporary Features

但 ; in 非但免過 "it is not merely that he avoids error" (7.85 (章)).

凡 ; in 車絕乎凡 "far removed from the commonalty" (7.85 (章)).

應 ; in 應得其里 "must get the underlying reason for" (8.54 (章)).

須 ; in 仁恩須人 "for humanity and kindness there needs to be human beings" (8.66 (章)).

See also 俱 u.f. 皆 (6.121 (章)).

APPENDIX 3

LATE HAN AND MODERN
STANDARD CHINESE

Karlgren, commenting on the occurrence of <u>tzay</u> 在 in the
<u>Luen Herng</u> (論衡) as a post-verbal particle, notes
that this is a feature of Modern Standard Chinese, and
describes its appearance as early as Han as "a remark-
able innovation."[1] A number of the innovations introduced in Late Han, following the Archaic-Han Shift,
anticipate usages current in Modern Standard Chinese,
of which the following are selected examples:

	LAC	Late Han	Modern Standard Chinese
不弗 } Mood	不	不
毋勿 } and	>	[無 for 有]	[沒 for 有]
無 } negation		negation only	negation only
		須 >	須要
		應 } >	應當
		當 }	
且 當 potential	>	且 momentary	暫且 "temp-
		暫 momentary >	orarily"
欲 "wish		欲 "wish" }	
		要 "wish" } >	要 {"wish"
		欲 "will" }	{"will"
既 }	>	已	> 已經
已 }			

---

[1] See Bernard Karlgren, "Excursions in Chinese
Grammar," <u>BMFEA</u> 23 (1951) p. 127, but on this, see also
<u>EAC</u> 3.4.5.1, footnote 26.

LAC	Late Han	Modern Standard Chinese
	但 "only" ⎫ "but" ⎭	但是 "but"
	即 "at once" 便 "at once"	立即 "at once" 便 "then"
見 (passive)	見 為 被 (蒙)	⎫ 見 被 蒙
於	於 在 >	在
自 ⎫ "self" ⎬ ⎭ "from"	> 自；自己 "self" > 從 "from"	自己 "self" 從 "from"
莫 (agential)	莫 negative	莫 negative (dial) cf. 沒
或 (agential)	> 或 … 或 … "either/or/" >	或是 "or"
孰 誰	⎬ 誰	誰
相 (reciprocity)	相 > parasitic	parasitic in, e.g., 相信 "believe"
他 日 今 日 明 日	昨 日 > 今 日 > 明 日	昨 天 今 天 明 天
因 故	> ⎰ 因：緣 ⎱ 故 > 緣 "deliberately"	⎰ 緣故 "reason" ⎱ 故意的 "deliberately"

LAC	Late Han	Modern Standard Chinese
	就使 "if" >	就是 "then"
	儻 "suppose"	倘若 (儻若)
		"even if"
最 太 }	before attribute	same
苐	for ordinals	same

JAW CHYI'S NOTIONS
ABOUT LANGUAGE

Throughout the <u>Commentary</u>, Jaw Chyi gives lexicographical glosses on words in the <u>Text</u> and from these we can deduce something of his ideas about language.

Lexicographical glosses usually take the form of providing synonyms or near synonyms (for example 茲此也 "the word <u>tzy</u> 'this' is <u>tsyy</u> 'this'" (5.86) or 亡猶無也 "the word <u>wang</u> ('not present') is similar to <u>wu</u> (also 'not present' in certain contexts)") (6.129), or are descriptive, as, for example, 庠序者教化之宮也 "<u>Shyang-shiuh</u> are buildings used for teaching" (1.28), 數罟密網也密細之網所以捕小魚鱉者也 "<u>Tsuh-guu</u> are <u>mih-woang</u>, that is fine-meshed nets, nets with which small fish and turtles are caught" (1.24).

But words are also placed in classes, of which Jaw Chyi distinguishes, <u>ming</u> 名; <u>cheng</u> 稱; <u>maw</u> 貌; <u>tsyr</u> 辭; and <u>sheng</u> 聲 or <u>in</u> 音.

<u>Ming</u> 名 serves to denote personal names as in 盆成 姓活名也 "P'en-ch'eng is the family name, K'uo the personal name" (8.88), but <u>ming</u> is also used for geographical names (for example 水名 "name of a river" (7.27); 地名 "place-name" (3.37)); and for the names of plants, for example 羊棗棗名也 "<u>yang-tzao</u> is the name of a date" (8.105). <u>Ming</u> is also used in 總名 for "generic name," as, for example, 械器之總名也 "<u>Shieh</u> is a general term for implements" (3.91).

<u>Cheng</u> is used for forms of address, particularly when such forms denote status, for example 公者國人尊君

之稱也 "<u>Gong</u> is a form of address used by subjects when showing deference to a prince" (3.39); 子男子之通稱也 "<u>Tzyy</u> is the common form of address to a male" (6.61); 叟長老之稱也猶父也 "<u>Soou</u> is a form of address to senior elderly people, rather like the use of <u>fuh</u> "father" " (1.5); 氓野人之稱 "<u>Min</u> is a way of referring to country folk" (3.83).

    <u>Maw</u> is used for words which describe things metaphorically, as they appear to be or give the impression of being. <u>Maw</u> is used literally in 有若之貌 "Yu-jo's physical appearance" (3.112) but, in an extended sense, <u>maw</u> describes the function of the class of reduplicate (xx, xx-<u>ran</u>, and x-<u>ran</u>, see <u>LAC</u> 3.3.3.1) which describe manner metaphorically. For this usage Professor Demiéville has coined the word "impressif". For example, 濯濯然無草木之貌 "<u>Jwo-jwo</u> (lit. "as though scrubbed") describes the appearance presented by a lack of vegetation" (6.102); 蟉蟉欲絕之貌 "<u>Lii-lii</u> describes the impression given by something about to snap off" (8.72); 訑訑者自足其智不嗜善言之貌 "<u>yi-yi</u> describes the impression given by one who thinks his own wisdom all-sufficient and has no liking for good advice" (7.56); 晬然潤澤之貌 "<u>Tsuey-ran</u> means giving the appearance of having been anointed" (i.e., glowing, suffused, shining - - as in "it appears, with a glow, on the face") (7.99); 囂囂自得無欲之貌 "<u>Shiau-shiau</u> means giving an impression of contentment, of having no desires" (7.81); 圉圉魚在水羸劣之貌 "<u>Yeu-yeu</u> (lit. "a corral" and thus "corralled") describes the appearance of a fish entangled in the water" (5.88); 赧赧然面赤心不征貌也 "<u>naan-naan-ran</u> means red in the face, it describes the appearance presented when all is not right in the heart" (4.38); 望望然慙愧之貌也 "<u>wanq-wanq-ran</u> describes the manner affected by one who feels mortified" (2.107).

Sheng 聲 and in 音 describe onomatopoeia, as, for
example, 填鼓音也 "tyan is the sound made by a drum"
(1.22); 閩鬭聲也 "honq is the hubbub of battle" (2.19).
In 2.53 施 in the name 孟施舍 is glossed as 發音也 "a
prefix marking phonetic attack."

Tsyr denotes a word in a very general sense. The
following are defined simply as tsyr: fwu 夫 (8.22); eel
爾 (5.85); wei 惟 (4.15); guh 固 (1.64); yueh 曰 (1.5);
chyh 翅 (7.4). Tann-tsyr 歎辭 "sigh-word" denotes an
interjection, as in 夫歎辭也 "Fwu is an interjection"
(6.64) and as in 於音烏歎辭也   "於 is pronounced
like 烏, it is an interjection" (7.3); and as in 惡者
不安事之歎辭 "U is an interjection expressing un-
ease" (2.74) (in 2.121 u is described as a deep sigh);
爾歎而不怨之辭 "Eel is an interjection but has no
suggestion of resentment" (8.123).

Tsyr is also used when a word is described by the
function it performs. For example 云爾絕語之辭也
"yun-eel are words that mark a break in speech" (2.121).
焉耳者怨至之辭 "The words yan eel are used to indicate emphatic finality" (1.20). Words with overtones
of status are called 謙辭, as for example 亦聖人之謙
辭 explaining the occurrence of chieh 竊 in the Text, "a
word indicating self-deprecation on the Sage's part"
(5.35), and in explaining 竊聞 in the Text: 故謙辭言
竊聞也 "And so, using self-deprecating words, he says
'chieh wen'" (3.75). Another way of referring to status
words is 君臣上下之辭 "words differentiating prince
and subject, superior and inferior," as in 1.10, where 國
"state" and 家 "estate" are said to belong to this class
of words.

Jaw Chyi thus distinguishes between "words" tsyr and
"non-words" sheng and in (i.e. onomatopoeic or non-phon-

emic sounds), and among "words" segregates names <u>ming</u>
- - both personal, proper, and generic names - -; social
appelations <u>cheng</u> which have to do with the social usage
of language; and words which describe manner <u>maw</u>.

Words are definable by replacement (with synonyms or
near synonyms), by description, or by function.

In linguistic terms Jaw Chyi is aware of the part
played by status in language, distinguishes between
phonemic and non-phonemic sounds, but apart from the
recognition of a class of proper names, of status forms,
and of a special form of attribute, regards the entire
lexicon as a single undifferentiated whole.

LIST OF WORKS MENTIONED

Chmielewski, Janusz
   "Notes on Early Chinese Logic (II)."
      Rocznik Orientalistyczny XXVl: 2 (1963) 91-105.

Dobson, W.A.C.H.
   Late Archaic Chinese: A Grammatical Study
      (Toronto, 1959).
   Early Archaic Chinese: A Descriptive Grammar
      (Toronto, 1962).
   "Studies in the Grammar of Early Archaic Chinese.
      I, The Particle WEI." T'oung Pao, 46 (1958)
      339-368.
   "Studies in the Grammar of Early Archaic Chinese.
      II, The Word JO." T'oung Pao, 47 (1959)
      281-293.
   "Towards a Historical Treatment of the Grammar of
      Archaic Chinese. I, Early Archaic Yüeh 越 >
      Late Archaic Chi 及." Harvard Journal of
      Asiatic Studies, 23 (1960) 5-18.
   "Studies in Middle Archaic Chinese. The Spring and
      Autumn Annals." T'oung Pao, 50 (1963) 221-238.
   "Word Classes or Distributional Classes in Archaic
      Chinese"; in L'Hommage à Monsieur Demiéville
      (in press)

Jiau Shyun 焦循
   Meng-tzyy Jenq-yih (孟子正義); in 國學基本
   叢書簡篇 Commercial Press (Shanghai, n.d.).

Karlgren, B.
   "Excursions in Chinese Grammar." Bulletin of the
      Museum of Far Eastern Antiquities, Stockholm,
      23 (1951) 107-133.

Karlgren, B.

Grammata Serica Recensa (Stockholm 1957).

Leu Shwu-shiang (呂叔湘)

Hann-yeu yeu-faa Luenn-wen Jyi (漢語語法論文集)
(Peking, 1955).

Yang Shuh-dar (楊樹達)

Tsyr Chyuan (詞詮) (Shanghai, 1928).

Yoshikawa Kōjirō (translated by Glen W. Baxter)

"The Shih-shuo Hsin-yü and Six Dynasties Prose
Style." Harvard Journal of Asiatic Studies, 18
(1955), 124-141.

Wang Shean (王顯)

"Shy-jing jong gen chorng-yan tzuoh-yonq shiang-
dang-de Yeou-tzyh shyh, Chyi-tzyh shyh, Sy-tzyh
shyh, her Sy-tzyh shyh 詩經中跟重言作用
相當的有字式，其字式，斯字式，合思字式
Yeu-yan Yan-jiou 語言研究 4 (1959), 9-43.

AN	安	Replacing 焉, 惡, 惡呼 and in Late Han	8.3.i
BEEN-YOU	李由	As replacement for 始	5.5.ii
BEY	被	As periphrastic passive	3.4.ii
		Deployment of	3.4.ii Note
BIANN	便	Aspectual Determinant "at once"	3.2.vi
BIANN	徧	See Appendix I	
BIH	必	In 必不, intensive negative	3.1.iii
		In 必須, "must have or be"	3.1.viii
		Before verbs: "decidedly, inevitably, of a certainty." Negated by 不 and 未 In 當必. Injunctive before verbs	3.1.viii Note
BU	不	As all-purpose negative in Late Han	3.1.i
		In 不須.	3.1.viii
		In "不/verb/pronoun or demonstrative"	3.6.i
		As Sentential Modal particle. (See also 5.4.i)	5.4.iii
		In 不復 as conjunction	7.1.i

CHARNG	常	As replacement for 固	3.1.v
CHERNG	誠	As Conditional Conjunction. Replaces 苟 and 信. As modal determinant replaces 信.	7.2.ii
CHIEE	且	In Momentary Aspect "for time being," "at that time." In Potential Aspect "about to." In 方 且：暫且.	3.2.i
		As Conjunction.	7.1
CHII	豈	As replacement for 莫	4.2.i
		As replacement for 惡	8.3.i
		As Interrogative in Late Han.	8.3.vii
CHIING	頃	In Time phrases.	5.5.ii
CHU	初	See Appendix I	
CHYI	其	Confused with 之	2.2.i
		As demonstrative "this, this sort of"	2.3.ii
		In 其實 and 其終	2.3.iii
		Before certain nouns = "other"	2.3.iv
		Relationship with 斯	2.3.iv Note
		As Agentive Pronoun	4.1.i
		Reduced role in anaphora. (See also 8.1.ii; Appendix I.)	5.3.i

DANG	當	As marker of the Injunctive Mood	3.1.vii
		As verb "assume responsibility for, take office as, be equal to, or adequate for"	3.1.vii Note ii
		In 當必	3.1.viii
		As Conditional Conjunction	7.2.iv
DANN	但	Before nouns, "only"	2.4.ii
		Before verbs, restrictive aspect"	3.2.iv
		As polar form of 不	3.2.v
		Dann and the adversative (see also 7.1.i)	3.2.v Note
		Dann and polarity	3.6.ii
		As copula, also in 非但 ; and 但為 (see also Appendix II)	6.1.i
DAY	迨	See Appendix I	
DEEI	得	As marker of the Injunctive Mood	3.1.iv
DEENG	等	In 何等	8.3.v
		As "et cetera"	9.2
DWU	獨	In 獨身	4.5.i
EEL	耳	As sentential modal particle in Late Han	5.4.i

EEL	爾	In 爾之 as determinative pronoun in Late Han	2.1.i
		Obsolete as agentive pronoun in Late Han	4.1.i
		As allegro form obsolete in Late Han (see also 8.1.i)	5.4:i
ERL	而	Reduction of role in Late Han	5.1.i
		Parasitic occurrence in Instrumental phrase	5.2.i
		As adversative and simple connective conjunction (see also Appendix I)	7.1.ii
ERL-YII-YIH 而已矣		Replacement by 也 or 耳	5.4.i
FAAN	反	As conjunction "on the contrary" (see also footnote 1, 7.1.iii)	7.1.iii
FANG	方	In Momentary Aspect, also in 方且	3.2.i
FARN	凡	In Late Han > "commonplace, ordinary" (see Appendix II)	2.4.i
FEEI	匪	See Appendix II	
FOOU	否	Obsolescent in Late Han in pregnant usage	5.4.ii
		As Interrogative Sentential modal particle (see also 5.4.i)	5.4.iii

FU	夫	Obsolete as allegro form in Late Han	5.4
FUH	復	In Iterative Aspect, in Durative Aspect, as verb = "revive, restore" in 新復 "newly," before numerals "a further," and in parasitic usage	3.2.ii
		As Conjunction	7.1.i
FWU	弗	Replacement by 不	3.1.i
		In "弗/verb/demonstrat- ive"	3.6.i
		(see Appendix II)	
GONG	躬	As Agential Distributive, also occurs in 躬身	4.5.i
GOA-REN	寡人	Obsolescent in Late Han	8.1.i Note
GOOU	苟	Obsolescent in Late Han as Conditional Con- junction	7.2.ii
GU	姑	Replacement by 且	3.2.i
GUEY	貴	Replacement for modal 有	3.1.vi
GUH	固	Obsolescence in modal role in Late Han and replacement by 常 and 素	3.1.v
		Confusion with 故 and 古	3.1.v Note
GUH	故	Confusion with 固 and 古	3.1.v Note
GUOO	果	Obsolescence in modal role in Late Han and replacement by 能 and 竟	3.1.v
		Use in 果毅	
		Glossed as 克	3.1.v Note

GUU	古	Confusion with 固,故	3.1.v
HAY	害	See Appendix I	
HER	何	Assimilates 奚,曷 and 胡	8.3.iv
		Expanded as 何等,何人 云何 etc.	
		Substitutes for 焉	8.3.i
		In 何由 "of what use?" (see also Appendix I)	8.3.v Note
HER	曷	Obsolescence in Late Han (see also Appendix I)	8.3
HU	乎	Obsolescence in Late Han as post-verbal particle	3.4.v
		Loss of precision in Late Han as final particle	5.4.i
HUOH	或	Obsolescence as Agential Distributive in Late Han. Occurrence in 或...或... formations (see also Appendix I)	4.2.i
HWU	胡	Obsolescence in Late Han	8.3
I	一	See Appendix I	
IN	因	Introducing causal clauses	6.2
ING	應	See Appendix II	
IOU	攸	See Appendixes I and II	
JANN	暫	Momentary aspect, also occurs in 暫且	3.2.i
JEA	假	In 假使 as Conditional Conjunction	7.2.i

JEE	者	As marker of causal clauses	2.5.i
JER	輒	As Aspect "on each occasion" also occurs in 每輒	3.2.vii
JIA	加	In the degrees of comparison	9.1
JIANN	見	In periphrastic passive Deployment of	3.4.i 3.4.ii Note
JIAU	交	Obsolescence in Late Han as marker of reciprocity: Assimilation by 俱	4.3.i
JIE	皆	As Agential Distributive, post-verbal collective, and encroachment 皆 by 俱 (see also Appendix I)	4.2.ii
JIE	偕	Obsolescence in Late Han and replacement by 俱	4.2.ii
JIH	既	Replacement by 已 As marker of subordinate clause in Late Han	3.2.ii 5.1.ii
JII	己	As Agent in 己自 As Emphatic and Reflexive Pronoun, also occurs in 己身, 己自, 自己 As replacement for 之	4.5.i 4.5.ii 8.1.ii
JINQ	竟	As replacement for 果 In Time phrases "finally"	3.1.v 5.5.ii

JINQ-BU	竟不	As intensive negative	3.1.iii
JIOW	就	As Conditional Conjunction and as verb "come or go"	7.2.v
JIOW	舊	Used for 故	3.1.v Note
JIU	俱	As Agential Distributive encroaches upon 皆	4.2.ii
		As post-verbal collective	4.2.iii
		Encroachment upon 交 as marker of Reciprocity (see also Appendixes I and II)	4.3.i Note
JU	諸	In blunted usage as anaphoric pronoun in Late Han	5.3.ii
		Obsolescence as allegro form in Late Han (see also Appendix II)	5.4.i
JY	之	Occurrence between pronoun and noun	2.1.i
		Confusion with 其	2.2.i
		Occurrence between attribute and noun	2.6.i
		Reduced role in anaphora (see also 4.1.i and 8.1.i)	5.3.i
JYH	至	In Degrees of Comparison	9.1
JYI	即	In aspect "at once"	3.2.vi
		As copula	6.1.iii
JYI	及	See Appendix I	

JYUE	厥	See Appendix I	
KEE	可	Modal function of (see also Appendix I)	3.1.ix
KEE	哿	See Appendix I	
KEH	克	Gloss for 果	3.1.v Note
LINQ	令	In periphrastic causative and permissive	3.4.iv
MEEI	每	In 每輒	3.2.vii
MENG	蒙	In periphrastic passive	3.4.ii
MII	靡	See Appendix I	
MOH	莫	As negative in blunted usage	3.1.ii
		Obsolescence as Agential Distributive (see also Appendix I)	4.2.i
NAE	乃	See Appendix I	
NENG	能	As replacement for 果	3.1.v
		Modal function of	3.1.ix
NINQ	寧	As verb "bring peace to," as Interrogative substitute "could, can?"	8.3.ii
PI	丕	See Appendix I	
PIH	譬	Occurrence in 譬如;譬若;譬猶 etc.	6.1.iv
PUU	普	See Appendix I	
RAN	然	Obsolescence in pregnant usage	5.4.ii

RU	如	As replacement for 由	3.5.ii Note
		As replacement for 而	5.1.i
		In 譬如	6.1.iv
		As Conditional Conjunction, also occurs in 如使	7.2.i
RUOH	若	As replacement for 由	3.5.ii Note
		As selective conjunction	4.2.i Note
		In 譬若	6.1.iv
RUU	汝	Determinative form of	2.1.i
		As Agential pronoun (see also 8.1.i)	4.1.i
SHANQ	尚	Injunctive in 尚當 etc.	3.1.vii
		Replaces 猶 as concessive conjunction	7.3.iii
		Following a noun = "even a" (see also Appendix II)	
SHEN	身	An Agential Distributive, also occurs in 自身; 身自 and 獨身	4.5.i
SHENN	甚	In the Degrees of Comparison	9.1
SHI	奚	Obsolescent in Late Han and replacement by 何, and 何為	8.3.iv
SHIANG	相	Marker of reciprocity, also in parasitic usage (see also Appendix I)	4.3.i

SHINN	信	Obsolescence as Conditional Conjunction in Late Han and replacement by 誠	7.2.ii
SHIU	須	As marker of Injunctive Mood, as verb "should have or be", and occurrence in 不須; and 必須 (see also Appendix II)	3.1.viii
SHIU	胥	See Appendix I	
SHIU-YU	須臾	In Time phrases	5.5.ii
SHU-WU	殊無	As Intensive Negative	3.1.iii
SHWEI	誰	Assimilates 孰 (see also Appendix I)	8.3.iii
SHWU	孰	Obsolescence in Late Han and assimilation into 誰 (see also 8.3.iii and Appendix II)	4.2.iv
SHYAN	咸	As Agential Collective in Late Han (see also Appendix I)	4.2.v
SHYH-YIH	是亦	As replacement for 而	5.1.i
SHYH	是	As demonstrative, in determinant usage with 之 (see also 6.1.i Note)	2.3.i
		As copula	6.1.i
SHYI	昔	Obsolescence in Late Han	5.5.i
SHYR	時	See Appendix I	

SHYY	使	In periphrastic caus-ative and permissive	3.4.iv
		As Conditional Conjunct-ion, also occurs in 如使; and 假使	7.2.i
SHYY	始	Defined as 本由	5.5.ii
SUH	素	As replacement for 固, used for "habitually, formerly"	3.1.iv
SUOO	所	See Appendix I	
SY	斯	Obsolescence as Determin-ative Demonstrative in Late Han	2.3.i
		Relationship with 其	2.3.iv Note
		"Attribute/Sy" inter-preted as reduplication	3.3.ii
		Obsolescence as Condit-ional Conjunction in Late Han (see also 8.2 and Appendix II)	7.2.iii
TA	他	Before nouns "other"	2.3.iv
		他日 replaced by 異日	5.5.ii
TAANG	儻	As Concessive Conjunct-ion, for required condition	7.3.ii
TING	聽	As verb "to let or allow"	3.4.iv
TSERNG	曾	As Interrogative Substi-tute in Late Han	8.3.viii

TSORNG	從	Replacement for 自	3.5.i
		Replacement for 由	3.5.ii
		(see also Appendix I)	
TSYY	此	In Determinant usage with 之	2.3.i
		As Conditional Conjunction	7.2.iv
		In 此物; 此人 and 此事 replacing 之	8.1.ii
TZAI	哉	See 5.4.i	
TZAI	載	See Appendix I	
TZAY	在	As post-verbal particle, also in 在於	3.4.v
		Use in EAC	3.4.v Note
TZENG	增	In the Degrees of Comparison	9.1
TZER	則	As replacement for 而	5.1.i
		In 則復 as conjunction	7.1.i
		As replacement for 斯 as Conditional Conjunction (see also Appendix I)	7.2.iii
TZUEY	最	As marker of superlative degree	9.1
TZWO	昨	In 昨日 "yesterday"	5.5.i
TZWU	卒	In Time phrases	5.5.ii
TZY	茲	See Appendix II	
TZYH	自	Replaced by 從	3.5.i
		As Agential Distributive, also occurring in 躬自; 自身 ; 身自;己身; 自己	4.5.i

TZYH		In word-formation, as "self"	4.5.i
		As Concessive Conjunction in Late Han (see also Appendixes I and II)	7.3.i
U, U-HU	惡：惡呼	As Interrogative Substitute obsolescent in Late Han and replaced by 安 or 何	8.3.i
WANG	亡	See Appendix I	
WEI	惟	See Appendix I	
WEI	為	Obsolescence of modal role	3.1.vi
		In periphrastic passive constructions	3.4.iii
		Deployment in periphrastic passive	3.4.iii Note
WEY	謂	Used for 為 in 以為，所以 ...為 and for 為 as a verb	4.4.i
WEY	未	Replacement by 不	3.1.i
		Replacement by 無 before 有	3.1.i Note
		Blunted usage of	3.1.ii
		Before verbs and numerals "not yet"	3.1.iv
		In "未/verb/pronoun" constructions	3.6.i
WEY JIAN	為間	Obsolescence in Late Han	5.5.ii

WOANG	往	Replaces 昔 in Late Han and used in 往者 and 往日 ·	5.5.i
WOO	我	In 我之 as determinative pronoun in Late Han	2.1.i
		As Agential form (see also 8.1.i) (see also Appendix I)	4.1.i
WU	吾	In 吾之 as determinative pronoun in Late Han	2.1.i
		Obsolescence as Agential pronoun (see also 8.1.i)	4.1.i
WU	無	Replacement by 不	3.1.i
		Negation for 有	3.1.i Note
		In "Wu/verb/pronoun" constructions	3.6.i
		As replacement for 莫 (see also Appendix I)	
WU	毋	See 3.1.i	
WUH	勿	Replacement by 不	3.1.i
		In blunted usage	3.1.ii
		In wuh/verb/pronoun constructions (see Appendix II)	3.6.i
YAN	焉	Blunting of usage as anaphoric pronoun in Late Han	5.3.ii
		As Interrogative replaced by 安	8.3.i

YAN	言	See Appendix I	
YE	邪	As general marker of the Interrogative in Late Han	5.4.i
YEE	也	In blunted usage	5.4.i
YEOU	有	Negation by 無	3.1.i Note
		Obsolescence as modal and replacement by 貴	3.1.iv
		Before an attribute, interpreted as reduplication of attribute	3.3.ii
		Replacement for 或 (see also Appendix I)	4.2.i
YEU	與	See Appendix I	
YI	宜	As injunctive before verbs	3.1.viii
YI-CHIEE	一切	As "momentarily"	3.2.i Note
YIH	已	For perfective aspect	3.2.ii
YIH	益	In the degrees of comparison	9.1
YIH	亦	As conjunction	7.1.i
YIH-RYH	異日	As replacement for 他日	5.5.ii
YII	矣	In blunted usage	5.4.i
YII	以	As replacement for 而 in Late Han (see also Appendix I)	5.1.i

YOU	由	Replacement by 從	3.5.ii
		Replacement by 如 and 若	3.5.ii Note
		Occurrence in 譬由	3.5.ii Note
		(see also 6.1.iv)	
		Obsolescence of modal role	3.5.ii Note
		Use as verb "to use, follow" and occurrence in 何由 for "of what use?"	3.5.ii Note
		(see also Appendix I)	
YOU	猶	Replaced by 復 for durative aspect	3.2.iii
		Obsolescent as Concessive Conjunction in Late Han and replacement by 尚	7.3.iii
YOW	又	Replacement by 復 for Iterative Aspect in Late Han	3.2.iii
		As conjunction occasionally replaced by 復 in Late Han	7.1.i
YU	于	Obsolescent in Late Han as post-verbal particle (see also Appendix I)	3.4.v
YU	與	Obsolescent as allegro form in Late Han	5.4.i
YU	於	As marker of the Locative	3.4
		Occurrence in 在於	3.4.v
		(see also Appendix I)	

YUAN	緣	Introducing causal clauses	6.2.i
		Before verbs "deliberate-ly, of set purpose"	6.2.i
YUAN	爰	See Appendix I	
YUEH	越	See Appendix I	
YUH	欲	In Potential Aspect "about to" and in Desiderative Aspect "wish to"	3.2.i
		Occurrence in 且欲 and 將欲	3.2.i
YUH	聿	See Appendix I	
YUN	云	In 云何 and as verb "to say"	8.3.v

Lightning Source UK Ltd.
Milton Keynes UK
UKHW030613210722
406167UK00006B/659